# MASTERING

# ENGLISH AS A
# FOREIGN LANGUAGE

# MACMILLAN MASTER SERIES

Accounting
Arabic
Astronomy
Australian History
Background to Business
Banking
Basic Management
Biology
British Politics
Business Communication
Business Law
Business Microcomputing
C Programming
Catering Science
Catering Theory
Chemistry
COBOL Programming
Commerce
Computer Programming
Computers
Economic and Social History
Economics
Electrical Engineering
Electronics
English as a Foreign Language
English Grammar
English Language
English Literature
Financial Accounting
French 1
French 2
German 1

German 2
Hairdressing
Human Biology
Italian 1
Italian 2
Japanese
Keyboarding
Marketing
Mathematics
Modern British History
Modern European History
Modern World History
Nutrition
Office Practice
Pascal Programming
Philosophy
Physics
Practical Writing
Principles of Accounts
Psychology
Restaurant Service
Science
Social Welfare
Sociology
Spanish 1
Spanish 2
Spreadsheets
Statistics
Statistics with your Microcomputer
Study Skills
Typewriting Skills
Word Processing

# MASTERING
# ENGLISH AS A
# FOREIGN LANGUAGE

## ROB NOLASCO

### EDITORIAL CONSULTANT
### BETTY PARR

MACMILLAN

First edition 1990
Reprinted 1991

Published by
MACMILLAN EDUCATION LTD
Houndmills, Basingstoke, Hampshire RG21 2XS
and London
Companies and representatives
throughout the world

Printed in Great Britain by
Billing & Sons Ltd, Worcester

Nolasco, Rob
Mastering English as a Foreign Language.—
(Macmillan Master Series)
1. Spoken English language
I. Title   II. Parr, Betty
428.3
ISBN 0–333–45877–X
ISBN 0–333–45878–8 Pbk
ISBN 0–333–45879–6 Pbk export

ISBN 0–333–46549–0 Audio cassette

# CONTENTS

*Background* – A British holiday
*Aims* – Learn to express possibility,
probability and future intentions
*Writing* – A letter of thanks

## II. REFERENCE MATERIAL 207

# SERIES EDITOR'S PREFACE

Mastering English as a Foreign Language, like all the other language courses in this series, is designed for adults working with or without a teacher. It is, however, not for beginners, but for students who already have a basic knowledge of English and wish to improve their command of the spoken and written language so that they may use it effectively in everday life. The book is accompanied by a cassette, which is an important element in the programme.

Though all the language skills are practised, the emphasis is on the spoken language of ordinary, educated people. The occasional introduction of American English is intended as a reminder of the wide spread use of the language, but it is not meant to serve as an alternative model.

The ground plan of the Course is similar to that in the other first-stage language books of the series. Each chapter begins with dialogues based on everyday situations, and this material provides the context for all the teaching. Explanations of vocabulary and grammar are followed by exercises graded at two levels. Exercises under A are based on the language of the dialogues but those under B go further and provide additional practice for students who want it. They can also assess their progress with the help of the key to the exercises, placed in the reference section at the end of the book. Each chapter contains background information, so that some insight may be obtained into different aspects of everyday life in England. In a book of this size, it. is unfortunately impossible to include details of the other countries in the United Kingdom.

The reference section contains, in addition to the key to the exercises, a guide to pronunciation and a summary of the grammar introduced throughout the book. There is a short bibliography as well as a list of useful addresses. It is hoped that the student will find this carefully planned course a helpful aid to study, which will bring the pleasure of an increasing mastery of the English language, with all its vigour and variety.

BETTY PARR

*Editorial Consultant*

# INTRODUCTION:

# HOW TO USE THIS BOOK

This course is for students of English as a Foreign Language. It is intended for those who speak some English but feel that it is now time to master the English used in everyday communication.

The story of a girl's visit to England provides the framework for a rapid revision of the main structures and vocabulary of English. There are practice exercises, background information about Britain, explanations of vocabulary and grammar, and a reference section. The reference section includes a Grammar Reference Section, a Guide to Pronunciation and an Answer Key. The course also comes with a cassette, a most important element in the programme.

## CHAPTER STRUCTURE

Each chapter starts with a series of dialogues.
Each dialogue is followed by explanations of:
1   Useful expressions and vocabulary
2   The main grammar points in the chapter
Next there is a simple background text about British life.
Then there are exercises.
The exercises in Section A are based on the dialogues in the chapter.
The exercises in Section B provide further practice, at a slightly more difficult level.
There is a short writing task at the end of each chapter.
Here are some ideas on how to use the different sections of the book:

## GUIDE TO PRONUNCIATION

This is a summary of the main sounds of English.
Try to listen to this as soon as you can.
Listen and repeat, using your pause button where necessary.

## DIALOGUES

These provide examples of spoken English.
If possible listen to the dialogue before you read the text.
This will help your listening.

When you have read the explanations and finished the exercises repeat the dialogues as you listen to the tape, using the pause button to give you time to practise.

## EXPLANATIONS

Try to see if you can understand the vocabulary and expressions without using a dictionary.
Learn the key expressions and use them if you get the chance.
Some learners find grammar explanations very helpful, others do not.
Don't worry if you find the explanations difficult. The important thing is to get the exercises right.

## BACKGROUND

The background texts give information about life in England.
When you read them try to use your knowledge of the world and your own country to help you understand them.
Underline any useful expressions and learn them.
The background texts will help your reading skills.
It is not possible, in a book of this size, to include any detailed references to the other parts of the United Kingdom.

## EXERCISES

If you are short of time concentrate on Section A.
Use the Answer Key to check your exercises.
If writing English is important to you then try the writing tasks.
In some cases there are model answers.

## GRAMMAR

This is a simple summary of some of the main grammar points.
Use it for revision.

## SOURCES OF INFORMATION

The bibliography and the addresses are provided to help you to get more information about England and English.

## SUPPLEMENTARY VOCABULARIES

This part of the reference section groups together some of the more important words in English. Learn them if you have time.
Some are in the book. Others are not.

Remember that we all learn languages in different ways, so use this book in a way that suits you and the time you have got for study.

Rob Nolasco

# I TEACHING UNITS

# ARRIVING IN BRITAIN

## 1.1 DIALOGUES 📼

### (a) Dialogue 1

Brigitte is at Heathrow Airport, London.

*Immigration Officer*:   Good morning. Could I see your passport, please?

*Brigitte*:   Er Good morning. Here you are!

*Immigration Officer*:   Ah, you're German . . .

*Brigitte*:   Yes.

*Immigration Officer*:   You're in the wrong queue . . .

*Brigitte*:   Queue?

*Immigration Officer*:   Yes, queue. You know, line . . . Like the people behind you. This queue is for non-EC passengers.

*Brigitte*: I'm terribly sorry . . .
*Immigration Officer*: It doesn't matter. Right, how long are you planning to stay, Miss Scherer?
*Brigitte*: Two weeks. I'm on holiday!
*Immigration Officer*: Fine, here's your passport! Welcome to Britain.

**(b) Dialogue 2**

A customs officer stops Brigitte in the green channel.
*Customs Officer*: Excuse me, miss . . . Can I see your passport, please?
*Brigitte*: Here you are.
*Customs Officer*: How long are planning to stay?
*Brigitte*: Two weeks; I'm on holiday.
*Customs Officer*: Right, you're in the green channel.
*Brigitte*: Yes . . .
*Customs Officer*: Do you have anything to declare? Any cigarettes? Alcohol?
*Brigitte*: No . . .
*Customs Officer*: Is this all your luggage? This case here?
*Brigitte*: Er yes, and the bag I'm carrying.
*Customs Officer*: Fine, that's all. Welcome to Britain.

### (c) Dialogue 3

*Taxi driver*: Is that all, one case?
*Brigitte*: Yes, I'm only here for two weeks.
*Taxi driver*: Get in . . . Where are you from?
*Brigitte*: Germany.
*Taxi driver*: Oh, yes, where . . .?
*Brigitte*: Koblenz. But I live near Düsseldorf now.
*Taxi driver*: My brother's in Germany.
*Brigitte*: Really?
*Taxi driver*: Yes, he's in the Air Force. He's a pilot . . .
*Brigitte*: How interesting . . .
*Taxi driver:* Oh yes, he really likes living there. . . Right; here we are . . . That's The Balmoral there. Let's see what we have on the meter. £18.50 please.
*Brigitte*: Here's £20. Keep the change . . .
*Taxi driver*: That's very kind. Here, I'll take your case.

## 1.2 VOCABULARY

### (a) Dialogue 1

(i) **Useful expressions**
I'm terribly sorry.
I'm on holiday.
How long are you
planning to stay?    (a Question for visitors)
Welcome to Britain!

(ii) **Words to learn**
Brigitte is German. Here is her passport.

West Germany is in the European Community (EC). A list of EC members is on page 11.

Queue
British English for a line of people, cars, *etc.* that are waiting.
A queue of people
A queue for coffee

**(b) Dialogue 2**

(i) **Useful expressions**
Do you have anything to declare?
or
Have you anything to declare?
Questions a Customs Officer asks.
Fine
Good,
OK
That's all!

(ii) **Words to learn**
Green channel
In the UK Customs, there is a red and green channel.
Green channel = nothing to declare
Red channel = goods to declare
luggage
Your cases, bags, *etc.*

**(c) Dialogue 3**

(i) **Useful expressions**
I'll give you a hand with your case. = I'll help you
You can use it to ask for help
Please give me a hand with the drinks.

Where are you from?
Possible answers:
Steffi Graf comes from Germany.
Mr Yamamoto's from Japan.
Really!
How interesting
These expressions encourage people to talk.
Keep the change

(ii) **Words to learn**
meter

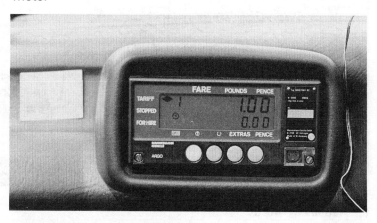

£18.50 (eighteen pounds fifty)

## 1.3 EXPLANATIONS

### (a) Verb 'to be'

| Positive | Negative | Interrogative |
|---|---|---|
| I am (I'm) | I am not (I'm not) | Am I . . . ? |
| You are (You're) | You are not | Are you . . . ? |
| He is (He's) | (You're not) | Is he . . . ? |
| She is (she's) | He is not (He's not) | Is she . . . ? |
| It is (It's) | *etc.* | Is it . . . ? |
| You are (You're) | | Are you . . . ? |
| We are (We're) | | Are we . . . ? |
| They are (They're) | | Are they . . . ? |

Brigitte is German.
She's from Stuttgart.
Laurent is French
He's from Paris.
Where is Hank from?
He's from San Francisco.
He's American.

**(b) This/That**

**(c) Nationality words**
Regular

| Country | Adjective | Person | Nation |
|---------|-----------|--------|--------|
| America | American | an American | the Americans |
| Germany | German | a German | the Germans |

Be careful with:

| | | | |
|---------|-----------|--------|--------|
| Greece | Greek | a Greek | the Greeks |
| China | Chinese | a Chinese | the Chinese |
| Japan | Japanese | a Japanese | the Japanese |
| Switzerland | Swiss | a Swiss | the Swiss |

| | | | |
|---------|-----------|--------|--------|
| Britain | British | a Briton | the British |
| France | French | a Frenchman | the French |
| | | a Frenchwoman | |
| Ireland | Irish | an Irishman | the Irish |
| | | an Irishwoman | |
| Scotland | Scottish | a Scot | the Scots |
| Spain | Spanish | a Spaniard | the Spanish |
| Sweden | Swedish | a Swede | the Swedish |
| Turkey | Turkish | a Turk | the Turks |
| Wales | Welsh | a Welshman | the Welsh |
| Italy | Italian | an Italian | the Italians |

## 1.4 **BACKGROUND**

### (a) **Arriving in Britain**
Great Britain = England, Scotland and Wales.
The United Kingdom = Great Britain and Northern Ireland.
Britain is an island. Visitors arrive by air and by boat. In the 1990s
there will be a Channel Tunnel.
London has two main airports–Heathrow and Gatwick.
Many visitors come by boat to ports like Dover and Southampton.

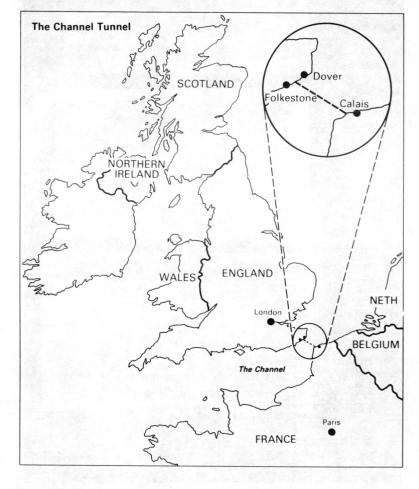

### (b) **Money**
The pound sterling is the currency used in the UK. (£)
One pound is one hundred pence.

£2.95 (two pounds ninety-five pence or two ninety-five)
A pound is also 0.454 kilograms.

## 1.5 EXERCISES

### Section A

### Exercise 1

You are Brigitte. Use the information in the dialogues above to fill in the blanks.

*Immigration Officer*: Excuse me, can I see your passport, please?
*Brigitte*: . . . . . . .
*Immigration Officer*: Ah, you're German. Where are you from?
*Brigitte*: . . . . . . .
*Immigration Officer*: That's nice. How long are you planning to stay?
*Brigitte*: . . . . . . .
*Immigration Officer*: What is your address in England?
*Brigitte*: . . . . . . .
*Immigration Officer*: Fine, welcome to Britain.

### Exercise 2

Complete these tables.

| EC Countries | |
|---|---|
| Name | Nationality |
| Germany | German |
| France | . . . . . . . |
| United Kingdom | . . . . . . . |
| Greece | . . . . . . . |
| Ireland | . . . . . . . |
| Spain | . . . . . . . |
| Portugal | . . . . . . . |
| Netherlands | . . . . . . . |
| Belgium | . . . . . . . |

| Some non EC Countries | |
|---|---|
| Name | Nationality |
| America | . . . . . . . |
| China | . . . . . . . |
| India | . . . . . . . |
| Japan | . . . . . . . |

### Exercise 3

Read these notices.

If you have nothing more than the allowances and no prohibited or restricted goods, or goods for commercial purposes, go straight through the green channel – unless you are asked to stop by an Officer.

If you have more than the allowances listed or if you have prohibited or restricted goods, or goods for commercial purposes, you must declare them to an Officer. Go into the red channel.

Within the allowance for alcohol

Over the allowance for alcohol

These are prohibited or restricted goods in the UK

He has goods for commercial purposes

Do this couple have anything to declare? Should they go to the red or green channel? Why?

## Section B

### Exercise 4
Match the people to the jobs.

| labourer pilot doctor businesswomen |
| --- |
| taxi-driver accountant nurse typist |
| engineer teacher soldier factory worker |

**Exercise 5**
Complete these statements.

My name's Brigitte.
I'm a tourist.
I'm from Koblenz.
I'm here on . . . . . . .
I'm planning to stay . . . . . . .

My name's . . . . . . .
I'm from San Francisco.
I'm an accountant.
I'm here . . . . . . .
I'm . . . . . . . two years.

My name's Laurent.
I'm from Paris.
I'm a . . . . . .
I'm here to study . . . . . . .
I'm planning to stay for twelve weeks.

**Exercise 6**
Complete these sentences with a form of 'to be'.
1 Manuel and Jose . . . . . . . Spanish; they . . . . . . . from
  Madrid.
2 Carlo . . . . . . . from Italy. He . . . . . . . an architect in New
  York.
3 . . . . . . . Peter and Paul English?
4 Where . . . . . . . you from?
5 . . . . . . . Hank an accountant or a student?

6 ....... this the queue for EC passports?
7 Switzerland ....... a member of the EC.
8 The Scherers ....... German.
9 They ....... students. They are tourists.
10 My address ....... the Balmoral Hotel, London.

**Writing**
Write a short description of yourself.
My name's .......
I'm from ....... (country)
I'm ....... (nationality)
I'm a ....... (profession)
My address is .......

# CHAPTER 2

# I HAVE A RESERVATION HERE

## 2.1 DIALOGUES 📼

### (a) Dialogue 1

Brigitte is in the Balmoral hotel.

*Receptionist*: Can I help you?

*Brigitte*: Yes, my name's Scherer. I have a reservation here?

*Receptionist*: Right, I'll just find the details. How do you spell it? S-H-E-R-E-R?

*Brigitte*: Er no, there's a C. S-<u>C</u>-H-E-R-E-R.

*Receptionist*: Ah yes! Here we are. A single room with bath for 13 nights.

*Brigitte*: Yes, that's right. How much is the room?

*Receptionist*: £60 a night including VAT. Are you here on business?

*Brigitte*: No, I'm on holiday?

*Receptionist*: Here's a form for you to complete. How are you going to pay?

*Brigitte*: By credit card. Visa.

Receptionist: Fine, it's room 205, on the second floor. Do you have a lot of luggage?

*Brigitte*: No, just this case here.

*Receptionist:* Um, please give me your card. I'll take the number and get the porter to take your bag and show you to your room.

### (b) Dialogue 2

Brigitte telephones reception from her room.

*Brigitte*: Hello, this is room 205. What time's dinner, please?

*Receptionist:* The main restaurant opens at 7 in the evening and last orders are at 10. Our coffee shop is open 24 hours a day.

*Brigitte*:   And what time is it now, please?
*Receptionist:*   It's 6 p.m.
*Brigitte*:   Thank you.

### (c) Dialogue 3

Brigitte is in the queue for the coffee shop. A waiter arrives.
*Waiter*:   Good evening.
*Brigitte*:   Have you got a table for one?
*Waiter*:   Certainly, come this way, please.

### (d) Dialogue 4

A little later. Hank is at the next table.
*Hank*:   Hi! My name's Hank Byam.
*Brigitte*:   Hello.
*Hank*:   Are you here on business?
*Brigitte*:   No, I'm on holiday.
*Hank*:   That's nice. I'm here on business. Is it your first visit to England?
*Brigitte*:   Yes. It is. And you?
*Hank*:   Yes. Me too! I like London. Where are you from?


## 2.2 VOCABULARY

### (a) Dialogue 1
#### (i) Useful expressions
Can I help you?
The receptionist says: Can I help you?
You can say to a taxi driver: Can you help me with my luggage, please?
I have a reservation

You can use this expression for a room in a hotel, a table in a restaurant or a seat in the theatre.
My name is Smith. I have
a reservation for
8 p.m.

- How do you spell it?
  Other examples:
  Apple is spelt A-P-P-L-E
  How do you spell Byam?
  My name is Zerkowitz. Shall I spell it for you?
- A single room with bath
  Single = for one person, a single room; a single bed
  A double room with shower
  A double = for two people; a double room; a double bed; a double ticket
  Do you have two doubles?
  A twin = a room for two people with two beds
- How much is the room?
  The ground floor
  The first floor
  The second floor

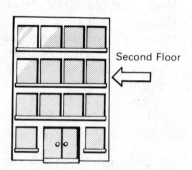

Second Floor

(ii) **Words to learn**
- a credit card
  Visa, Access, Mastercharge, *etc*. are all credit cards.
- a form (see page 24 for an example)
- a receptionist
  When you arrive in an hotel you go to reception where there is a receptionist.
- a porter

## (b) Dialogue 2

### (i) useful expressions

- What time's dinner? = What time is dinner?
  You can ask: What time is the bank open?
  Banks usually open at 9:30.
  Banks close at 3 p.m.

- What time is it?
  It's just after six.
  You can also use: What's the time now?
  or
  Can you tell me the time?

## (c) Dialogue 3

### (i) Useful expressions

- Have you got a table?
  You can also say: Have you got a double room?
  Certainly = Of course. Yes.
  A:  Can you carry my case?
  B:  Certainly.

## (d) Dialogue 4

### (i) Useful expressions

- Hi! My name's. . .
  Hi (Informal) = Hello!
- Is this your first visit?
  Me too!
  A:  I'm German.
  B:  Me too! = B is German
  A:  I'm here on business.
  B:  Me too! = B is on business.

## 2.3 EXPLANATIONS

### (a) Time

These examples show ways of saying the time.

three o'clock                three in the morning
three                        3 a.m. (03:00)

three in the afternoon
3 p.m. (15:00)

9 a.m.
nine in the morning          09:00

9 p.m.
nine in the evening
nine at night                21:00

Midday or noon = 12:00
Midnight = 00:00

a quarter past one
quarter past one             1:15
one fifteen

twenty-five past two
twenty-five minutes past two    2:25
two twenty-five

half past ten
ten-thirty                   10:30
half ten

a quarter to twelve
quarter to twelve            11:45
eleven forty-five

ten to nine
ten minutes to nine          8:50
eight-fifty

Office hours are from 9 a.m. to 5 p.m.
At three in the morning he was in his room.
Dinner is at seven-thirty.

**(b) Introductions**
Greetings
Hello. Hi! (very informal)
Good morning/afternoon/evening (more formal)
When someone introduces you, you can answer:
Hello! (informal) or How do you do? (formal)
*Hank*:   Brigitte, this is Laurent.
*Brigitte*:   Hello!
*Laurent*:   Hello! Is this your first visit? . . .

*Hank*:   Mrs Smith, may I introduce Brigitte Scherer?
*Brigitte*:   How do you do?
*Mrs Smith*:   How do you do? Is this your first visit? . . .

How do you do? is a polite greeting. You don't need to answer the question.
You can also use: Pleased to meet you in a first meeting.
*Hank*:   Brigitte, this is Laurent.
*Brigitte*:   Pleased to meet you.
This is polite.

**(c) Have got**
In British English: I have got = I have
It is a present tense.
I have not got (I haven't got) is negative.
Have I got? is the question form.

## 2.4 BACKGROUND

**(a) Bed and Breakfast**
In Britain, Bed and Breakfast is a system where you pay for a room and breakfast the next morning. Some small hotels or guest houses are called a *Bed and Breakfast*. (B & B)
In the country you may find a room in an inn. An inn is a small old hotel, which usually has a pub. (see page 54)

**(b) 24-hour clock**
In Britain, the twenty-four hour clock is used in timetables.

Cambridge to London

| Depart | Arrive |
|--------|--------|
| 17.05  | 18.05  |

*etc.*
Very few people use it in conversation.

**(c) VAT**
VAT is the British abbreviation for the 'value added tax' used in the European Community. Prices in restaurants, hotels and shops are usually inclusive of VAT (with VAT).

22

## 2.5 EXERCISES

**Section A**

**Exercise 1**
Complete these dialogues.

   1  *Receptionist*:   .......?
      *Brigitte*:   ....... a single room with bath?
      *Receptionist*:  Certainly.

   2  *Brigitte*:   ....... a reservation.
      *Receptionist*:  What .......?
      *Brigitte*:  Scherer.
      *Receptionist*:  How .......?
      *Brigitte*:  S-C-H-E-R-E-R.

   3  *Brigitte*:  What time is dinner?
      *Receptionist*:  Dinner is at seven in .......

**Exercise 2**
Complete these examples.
15:01                        It's one minute past three.

   1  18:53              It's six .......
                        It's ....... to .......

   2  05:13              It's thirteen .......
                        It's .......

   3  06:30              It's six .......
   4  07:45              It's .......

**Exercise 3**
Write out the times in English.

## Section B

### Exercise 4

You are Brigitte. Complete this form.

---

Surname: ................................................................

FirstName(s): ............................................................

Address: *Kennedystrasse 8, Koblenz, Germany*

Nationality: ..............................................................

Passport number: *92345*

Date of arrival: *8 July*

Date of departure: *29 July*

Method of payment: ....................................................

....................................................................

For office use only:

Type of accommodation: Single room with bath

Room number: 205

---

### Exercise 5

Write in the description for each of these types of room.

Follow the first example.

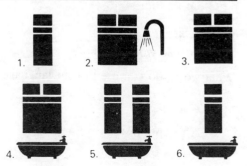

1: A single room

**Exercise 6**

These people work in a hotel

What words do you use in your language?

1  A manager

2  A receptionist

3  A porter

4   A cashier

5   A waiter

6   A chambermaid

**Exercise 7** 📠
The English alphabet is on page 275.

Listen to how the letters are pronounced.

Learn to spell your name and address.

**Writing**
Complete the opposite form with your own personal information.

# CHAPTER 3

# WHERE IS THE TUBE STATION?

## 3.1 DIALOGUES 📼

### (a) Dialogue 1

Brigitte is in the hotel.

*Hank*: Hi! Brigitte. How are you?

*Brigitte*: Fine, thanks, and you?

*Hank*: I'm very well. Brigitte, these are my friends Laurent and Seiki. Laurent is a student from France and Seiki's from Japan. He's on business too.

*Brigitte*: How do you do?

*Laurent*: How do you do?

*Seiki*: Hello.

### (b) Dialogue 2

*Brigitte*: Is there a tube station near the hotel?

*Hank*: Oh, yes. There's one on the corner of Kensington High Street and Derry Street. When you leave the hotel turn left. The subway, er sorry, underground station is about five hundred yards away on the right.

### (c) Dialogue 3

*Brigitte*: Excuse me, where's the tube station?

*Stranger*: It's in front of you, miss! Next to the department store.

*Brigitte*: Oh!

### (d) Dialogue 4

*Brigitte*: Excuse me. Can you tell me the way to the Houses of Parliament, please?

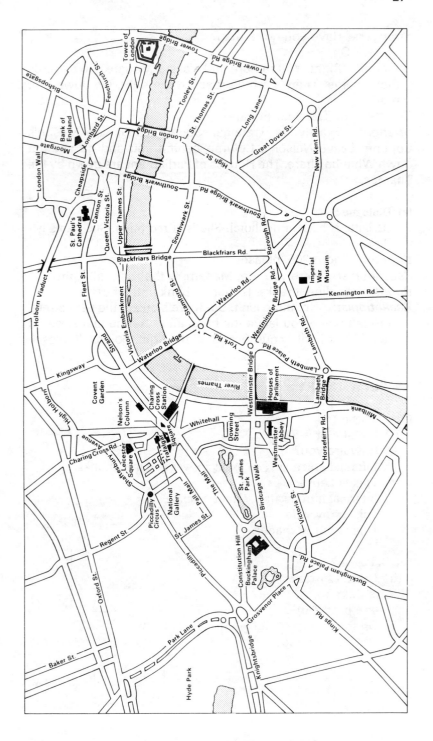

*Stranger*: Have you got a map?

*Brigitte*: Oh, yes.

*Stranger*: Right. You're here, in Leicester Square. Go towards that cinema. There's a little road on the right. Go down that road.

*Brigitte*: To Trafalgar Square?

*Stranger*: Exactly. In Trafalgar Square you'll see Nelson's Column. Leave Nelson's Column behind you and go straight down Whitehall here. The Houses of Parliament are down by the Thames.

**(e) Dialogue 5**

Brigitte is back in the hotel. She is at reception. She wants her key.

*Brigitte*: Room 205, please.

*Receptionist*: Here you are, Madam. Is the room all right?

*Brigitte:* Er, fine, thanks. Is there a bank in the hotel?

*Receptionist*: No, there isn't. But there's one in the next street. Turn left when you leave the hotel and take the first street to the left. The bank is number 83 on the right. You can't miss it.

## 3.2 VOCABULARY

**(a) Dialogue 1**

　(i) **Useful expressions**

- How are you?
  Informal greeting. The usual answer is: Fine, thanks.
- This is Laurent.
  Informal introduction. Other examples:
  This is my wife.
  This is our Manager.

**(b) Dialogue 2**

　(ii) **Useful expressions**

- Is there a . . .?
  (see page 250)
- On the corner of Kensington High Street and Derry Street.

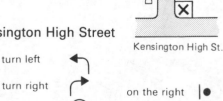

turn left
turn right
turn round
on the right
on the left

(ii) **Words to learn**
- tube or underground
  The tube is a word for the underground railway in London. In American English subway is used.
- 500 yards away
  1 yard = 3 feet or 36 inches or 91.4 centimetres.

## (c) Dialogue 3

(i) **Useful expressions**
- Excuse me
  In English we do not use words like Monsieur or Sir when we want attention. We use Excuse me.
  We use this expression before we talk to someone.
  Excuse me, is there a restaurant here?
  It does not mean I'm sorry
- In front of
- Next to

## (d) Dialogue 4

(i) **Useful expressions**
- Can you tell me the way to . . ., please?
  Polite way of asking: Where is . . .?
- Go straight down

(ii) **Words to learn**
Map
Cinema
(for towards, behind, etc. see page 250)

## (d) Dialogue 5

(i) **Useful expressions**
- Room 205, please.
  To ask for a key in a hotel you say the room number + please.
- Is the room all right?
  This means: Is the room good?
  Her answer was: Fine thanks. You can say: Well, there's a problem in the room.
  complaints, *etc.*(see Chapter 15)
- You can't miss it.
  It is easy to find.

### 3.3 EXPLANATIONS

#### (a) Imperatives
Imperatives = verb form without **to**. One use is for instructions and directions.
Go straight ahead.
Turn right (left).
Walk for 500 yards.
Take the second road to the left.

The negative form is made with **don't** or **do not**.
Don't turn left at the Church. Go straight on.

#### (b) Prepositions
Prepositions which say where something is (place)

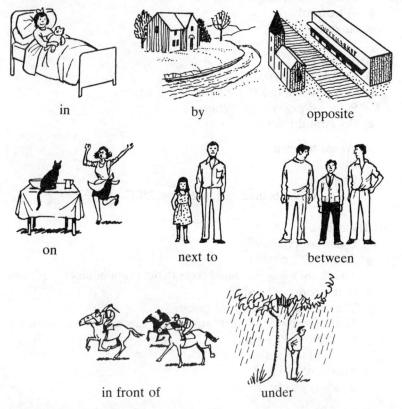

in

by

opposite

on

next to

between

in front of

under

To find the right use of a preposition you need a good dictionary.
Learn these examples.

at
She is at the tube station.
I live at 23 Kensington Street.
They are at the cinema.

in
She's in the garden.
I live in Kensington Street.
Brigitte is in London.

on
London is on the Thames.
He lives in Strasbourg on the border of France and Germany.

by (near to)
The Houses of Parliament are by the Thames.
She is by the door.
Prepositions which say where something is going (movement).

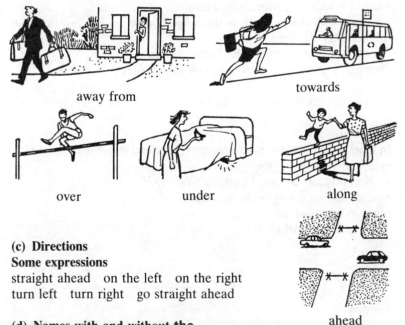

away from

towards

over

under

along

ahead

**(c) Directions**
**Some expressions**
straight ahead   on the left   on the right
turn left   turn right   go straight ahead

**(d) Names with and without the**
Why do we say: The Tower of London but Trafalgar Square?
Look at these examples:
at London University   at the University of London
in Parliament   in the Houses of Parliament
We use the before phrases with of.

Note these examples of places with the
1 The UK, the USSR, the USA, *etc.* (Plurals)
2 The Thames, the Seine, the Atlantic Ocean, the Grand Canal, *etc.*
  (rivers, seas and canals)
3 The Ritz, The Odeon, The British Museum (hotels, cinemas,
  theatres, *etc.*)
Note examples where we do not use the with places
1 Africa, Europe (continents)
2 England, India (countries)
3 Lake Windermere, Mount Everest (lakes and mountains)
4 London, Oxford, Fulbourn (cities, towns, villages)
5 Oxford Street, Piccadilly Circus, Tower Bridge (streets, places,
  *etc.*)
6 Buckingham Palace, Westminster Abbey, Victoria Station,
  Heathrow Airport (buildings that are not hotels, theatres, *etc.*

**(e) There is/are**
There (+ to be) = something exists
We start with there which is the subject of to be but put the 'real'
subject after the verb.
There is a restaurant in the hotel. (singular)
There are three banks in the building. (plural)

We can use all the tenses of to be (there was, there has been, *etc.*)

**(f) Addresses**
In England we use the house number, then the street name, the town
and finally the postcode.
23 Kensington Street, London, SW1 3XN
Sometimes we use only the number.
I live in number 53.
The bank is number 215.

## 3.4 BACKGROUND

### London
London has a population of about 7 million people. That is 13% of
Britain's population.
London has different centres.
The City (spelt with a capital C) is the financial and business centre.
St Paul's Cathedral and The Tower of London are in the City.
The West End is the area from the Mall to Oxford Street. It is the

centre for cinemas, theatres, clubs, and shopping. A popular area of the West End is Soho. London's China Town is in Soho. There are many bars and clubs as well as shops and restaurants from many different countries.

Westminster is the centre of government. 10 Downing Street, the Prime Minister's residence, is in Westminster. Westminster Abbey is opposite the Houses of Parliament.

The London Underground or tube has nine lines; there are many stations in Central London.

## 3.5 EXERCISES

### Section A

### Exercise 1
Put in the missing words and then put the sentences in the right order.
'Yes. It's . . . . . . . the hotel. Go . . . . . . . for about three hundred . . . . . . . ' ' . . . . . . . Is there a . . . . . . . near here.'
'Thank you very much.'
'The bank is . . . . . . . '

> yards  bank  next to  straight ahead  excuse me  on the left

### Exercise 2
Look at this list of places in London. Write in the where it is needed. The first example is complete.

The Houses of Parliament
. . . . . . . Tower of London
. . . . . . . Charing Cross Station
. . . . . . . Piccadilly Circus
. . . . . . . Buckingham Palace
. . . . . . . Imperial War Museum
. . . . . . . Bank of England
. . . . . . . Hyde Park

### Section B

### Exercise 3
In London visitors can travel by bus, by taxi, by tube or underground and by train but many go on foot.
Make a similar sentence about your town.

**Exercise 4**

There are many famous places and monuments in London. Where are they?

Nelson's Column is in Trafalgar Square.

Parliament is by the Thames.

Leicester Square is near Piccadilly Circus.

Use the map to help you make similar sentences about these places.

1 Westminster Abbey  2 St. Paul's Cathedral  3 The Tower of London  4 Downing Street

Now make similar sentences about places in your town.

**Exercise 5**

Answer these questions.

  (i) Is there an underground in your town?

 (ii) Is there an opera? Where is it?

(iii) Is there a railway station? Where is it?

(iv) Is there a science museum? Where is it?

 (v) Are there any Chinese restaurants? How many?

**Writing**

Look at the map on page 27.

Write simple instructions for a friend on how to go from:

  1 Piccadilly Circus to 10 Downing Street.

  2 Leicester Square to Oxford Street.

# I'D LIKE TO CHANGE SOME MONEY

## 4.1 DIALOGUES

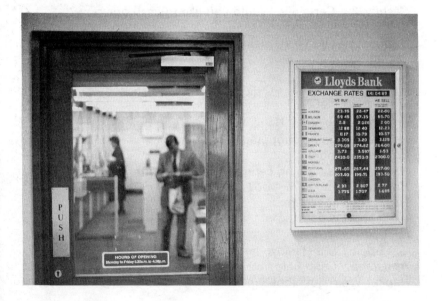

### (a) Dialogue 1

Brigitte is inside the bank near her hotel. She goes up to a cashier.

*Brigitte*: Excuse me, I'd like to change some traveller's cheques. What is the exchange rate for the Deutschmark against the pound?

*Cashier 1*: Ah! You want the foreign desk. Over there on the left.

**(b) Dialogue 2**

Brigitte goes to the foreign exchange window.

*Cashier 2*:   Can I help you?

*Brigitte*:   Er yes, I'd like to change some traveller's cheques, please.

*Cashier 2*:   Certainly, madam. How many do you want to change?

*Brigitte*:   Three please . . . 150 marks.

*Cashier 2*:   Fine. Please, sign them at the top. Could I have your passport please?

*Brigitte*:   Here you are . . .

*Cashier 2*:   Right. Here's your money and your passport. Enjoy your stay in England.

*Brigitte*:   Just one question. Do you cash Eurocheques in this bank?

*Cashier 2*:   Certainly. Would you like to cash one now?

*Brigitte*:   No, thanks. Not today!

*Cashier 2*:   OK. Next, please!

**(c) Dialogue 3**

When Brigitte leaves the bank she meets Hank.

*Hank*:   Hi!

*Brigitte*:   Oh, hello, Hank. Where are you going?

*Hank*:   I'm going shopping.

*Brigitte*:   Where?

*Hank*:   In a shopping centre round the corner.

*Brigitte*:   Can I come too?

*Hank:*   Sure! Where . . .

**(d) Dialogue 4**

Brigitte and Hank go into a souvenir shop.

*Assistant*:   Can I help you?

*Hank*:   We're just looking.

**(e) Dialogue 5**

Brigitte and Hank go into a boutique.

*Assistant*:   Can I help you?

*Hank*:   Yes, I'm looking for a blouse for my wife.

*Assistant*:   Here's a lovely one.

*Hank*:   What size is it?

*Assistant*:   Size 14.

*Hank*:   How much is it?

*Assistant*:   £15.99

*Hank*: Well, Brigitte. What do you think?
*Brigitte*: Er, blue doesn't suit me. I like the yellow one.
*Hank*: My wife likes blue. OK. I'll take it.
*Assistant*: How would you like to pay for it?
*Hank*: Cash.
*Assistant*: Fine. Come this way.

### (f) Dialogue 6

Brigitte is in a shoe shop.

*Brigitte*: Excuse me! Can I try that shoe on, please?
*Assistant*: This one?
*Brigitte*: No, that one. The black shoe.
*Assistant*: Certainly. What size are you?
*Brigitte*: 38.

The assistant brings the shoes.

*Assistant:* Here you are, Madam. Try these.
*Brigitte*: These are a bit small. Have you got them in a larger size?
*Assistant*: No. I'm afraid I haven't got them in black. Would you like to try these in brown?
*Brigitte*: Er, no thanks.

## 4.2 VOCABULARY

### (a) Dialogue 1

#### (i) Useful expressions

- Can I help you?
  Often used in shops, banks, *etc.*
- I'd like to = contraction of: I $\begin{array}{c}\text{would}\\\text{should}\end{array}$ like to
  means: I want to
- To change (some money, traveller's cheques, dollars, *etc.*)
  To give an amount of money from one country for the money of another country.
- Do you change traveller's cheques?

#### (ii) Words to learn

- Cashier
  The person that you pay or get money from in a bank, hotel, shop, *etc.*

traveller's cheque (traveler's check in American English)

| | |
|---|---|
| Exchange rate | What are the rates today? |

Here are the exchange rates.

## (b) Dialogue 2

### (i) Useful expressions

- Do you cash Eurocheques?
  To cash a cheque = to exchange a cheque for money
  I cashed a £50 cheque at the bank this morning.
- How many . . . ?
  (see explanation on page 40)
- Please sign them at the top.
  To sign = write your name.
- Here you are . . .
  You say: here, here's or here you are when you offer or give something to someone.
  *A:* That is my bag.
  *B:* Here you are.
  Enjoy your stay (holiday, *etc*)
  One way to end a conversation.

## (c) Dialogue 3

### (i) Useful expressions

    *Q:* Where are you going?
    *A:* I'm going shopping.
(see explanation on page 255)
Sure.
Informal way of saying: yes. Common in American English.
= certainly

### (ii) Words to learn

Shopping = activity of going to shops and buying things.
I'm going shopping in Oxford Street.

Who is going to do the shopping?
Shopping centre
Place in town where there are lots of shops together.

## (d) Dialogue 4

### (i) Useful expressions
We're just looking (or I'm just looking)
Use this expression when you don't want an assistant to help you in a shop.

### (ii) Word to learn
souvenir
Tourists often buy souvenirs. There are some on page 191.

This table is a souvenir from Morocco.
I would like a souvenir of this evening.

## (c) Dialogue 5

### (i) Useful expressions
- What size is it?
  How big or how small a thing is.
  Also a shop assistant may ask: What size do you take?
- How much is it?
- What do you think?
- It suits you.
  If something suits you, you look attractive in it.
  The dress suits you.
  Yellow doesn't suit you.

### (ii) Words to learn
Blouse = shirt for a girl or woman
Cash = coins or paper money. Not a cheque.
Q: How much cash do you have?
A: Only £10.00.
I paid for the hotel in cash.

## (f) Dialogue 6

### (i) Useful expressions
- Can I try this . . . on, please?
  to try on = put on clothing to see if it fits, suits you, *etc.*
- She tried on a new dress.
- Wait a moment = wait a short time.
- A bit small
  A bit = a little
  Her shoes are a bit small.

## 4.3 EXPLANATIONS

### (a) I'd like to + infinitive
In conversation 'd is a contraction of would or should. Would is a conditional.
(see page 265)
It is used with like, prefer, etc. to make polite offers or requests.
Would you like a cup of tea?
I would like to try this on, please.

### (b) Much/Many
Many is used with, countable or plural nouns.
many blouses   many hotels   many people
Much is used with uncountable or singular nouns.
much time   much money   much tea
Much and many are used mainly in negative sentences and questions.
There aren't many hotels.
Have you got many friends?
I haven't got much time.
In informal statements we often use a lot of or lots of with singular or plural nouns.
I have a lot of money. (Not: I have much money)
*Note*
There is lots of tea. Not: There are lots of tea
With lots of the verb is singular when there is a singular subject.

### (c) Some
With plural or countable nouns, some = a number of
some traveller's cheques = a number of traveller's cheques
some people = a number of people
We can also use some with uncountable nouns like money when we are not interested in how much.
some money = a certain amount of money.

### (d) Present continuous
Form

| Positive | Negative | Interrogative |
|----------|----------|---------------|
| I am looking<br>You are looking<br>She is looking | I am not looking<br>You are not looking<br>She is not looking | Am I looking?<br>Are you looking?<br>Is she looking? |

In conversation we use these contractions:

I'm  
He's/she's/it's              looking  
we're/you're/they're

We use the present continuous tense to talk about:
(i) Something which is happening at the time of speaking.
   **Where are you going? I'm going shopping.**
   **Can I help you? I'm just looking.**
   or
   Something that is happening around the time of speaking.
   **Laurent is learning English in the UK.** (He may not be studying at the moment).
(ii) We also use the present continuous to talk about changes.
   **Prices are rising every day.**
   **Laurent's English is getting better.**

**(e) One**

We often use one instead of repeating a singular noun.
**I'm looking for a blouse. I'd like a yellow one.**
*Note*
We use a when an adjective comes before one.
Normally there is no article.
**Give me one more.**
The plural is the ones.
**I want some shoes. Give me the ones in the window.**

## 4.4 BACKGROUND

**(a) Changing money**

In Britain tourists can change money at airports, banks, hotels, some tourist offices, travel agents or a money exchange. The rate of exchange is shown on a board. The rate can be different from place to place so check the rate in a bank or newspaper. However, you should always ask:
How much do you charge?
Sometimes these charges can be very high!

**(b) Going shopping**

English shoe and clothing sizes are different from European and American sizes.
In many shops you can ask to try shoes and clothing on. If you

cannot, you can usually try these at home and return the goods if they are the wrong size. Keep your receipts.

There is more information on shops and shopping on page 147.

## 4.5 EXERCISES

### Section A.

### Exercise 1

Put in the missing words and arrange the sentences in the right order.

Here's a nice . . . . . . .

Yes, please. I'm . . . . . . . for a blouse.

. . . . . . . What . . . . . . . are you?

Can I . . . . . . . you?

Fourteen.

I'm afraid yellow doesn't . . . . . . . me. Have you got a blue . . . . . . .?

Here, . . . . . . . this one on.

```
looking   one   help   certainly   size   suit   one   try
```

### Exercise 2

Complete the missing sections of these dialogues.

*A*: Good morning, . . . . . . . . . . . . .

*B*: How much do you want to change?

*A*: Excuse me, . . . . . . . . . . . . .

*B*: It's a size sixteen.

*A*: Can I . . . . . . . a size fifteen, please?

*B*: Of course, madam. . . . . . . . you are.

*A*: I'm sorry, the yellow blouse doesn't suit me.

*B*: Would you . . . . . . . try a blue . . . . . . .?

*A*: Yes, please.

### Exercise 3

Put the verb in the correct form. The first example has been done for you.

What are you doing? I'm **speaking** (to speak) to my mother.

Where are you? I . . . . . . . (to be) in the bedroom. I . . . . . . . (to try on) a new shirt.

Can you help us? We . . . . . . . (to look for) the Balmoral hotel.

Where's Brigitte? She . . . . . . . (to change) money at the cashier.
Where are you going? I . . . . . . . (to go) shopping. Do you want to come too?
Hi! Where's Hank? He . . . . . . . (to buy) a blouse for his wife.

## Section B

### Exercise 4

Complete these sentences with much, many and a lot of. Sometimes there are two answers. The first two have been done for you.
How much money do you have?
There are many people in the hotel.

1 There aren't . . . . . . . people in the restaurant.
2 There isn't . . . . . . . time before dinner.
3 There are . . . . . . . American tourists in London.
4 Do you have . . . . . . . tourists in winter?
5 How . . . . . . . coffee have you got?
6 This hotel is very quiet. It hasn't got . . . . . . . rooms.
7 How . . . . . . . cases do you have?

### Writing

Look at Brigitte's shopping list. It has some presents she wants to buy in London.

Now write a similar list for each member of your family.

# CHAPTER 5

# COULD YOU TAKE OUR ORDER, PLEASE?

## 5.1 DIALOGUES 📼

### (a) Dialogue 1

Brigitte and Hank go to the hotel restaurant.

*Hank*: Good evening.

*Waiter*: Good evening, sir. Have you got a reservation?

*Hank*: No. I'm afraid not. Have you got a table for two?

*Waiter*: Yes, sir. Over there by the window. Come this way, please.

Brigitte and Hank sit down at the table.

*Waiter*: Would you like something to drink?

*Brigitte*: Could I have a pint of beer, please?

*Waiter*: Certainly, madam. Would you like bitter or a lager?

*Brigitte*: Er, lager, please.

*Hank*: I'll have one too. Could you bring us the menu, please, we're hungry!

### (b) Dialogue 2

Brigitte and Hank are discussing the menu on page 45.

*Brigitte*: I think, I'll have the soup to start with. I like tomato. How about you?

*Hank*: No, I don't really like soup in summer. I'll have the mushrooms, followed by the steak . . .

*Brigitte*: I don't really like red meat. I think I'll have the chicken. Would you like some bread?

*Hank*: Yes, please. Now where is . . .

**(c) Dialogue 3**

The waiter returns.

*Waiter*:  Are you ready to order?

*Brigitte*:  Yes, I'd like to start with tomato soup and then I'll have the roast chicken, please.

*Waiter*:  Would you like a little cream in the soup?

*Brigitte*:  Yes please.

*Waiter*:  And you sir?

*Hank*:  I'd like the mushrooms, followed by the steak.

*Waiter*:  How would you like your steak?

*Hank*:  Medium, please.

*Waiter*:  Would you like wine with your meal?

*Hank*:  I'll have another beer, please. How about you, Brigitte? Would you like a glass of wine?

*Brigitte*:  No thanks. I'm all right.

---

❖❖❖❖❖❖❖❖❖❖❖❖❖❖❖❖❖❖❖❖❖❖❖❖❖❖❖❖❖❖❖❖❖❖❖❖❖❖❖❖❖❖❖❖

## *SPECIAL DINNER MENU*

### Starters
*Tomato soup*
*Mushrooms in cheese sauce*
*Prawn cocktail (£2.00 extra)*

### Main Course
*Fried fillet of plaice*
*Roast chicken with special stuffing*
*Grilled rump steak*
*Steak and kidney pie*
*Pork and apple casserole*
*All main courses are served with a choice of vegetables*

### Dessert
*Strawberries and cream*
*Lemon meringue pie*
*Apple tart*
*Cheese and biscuits*

❖❖❖❖❖❖❖❖❖❖❖❖❖❖❖❖❖❖❖❖❖❖❖❖❖❖❖❖❖❖❖❖❖❖❖❖❖❖❖❖❖❖❖❖❖❖❖

**(d) Dialogue 4**

Brigitte and Hank are eating their meal.

*Waiter*: Is everything all right?

*Hank*: It's excellent, thank you?

*Waiter*: Would you like more vegetables?

*Brigitte*: No, thanks.

*Hank*: I'll have a few French fries, please.

**(e) Dialogue 5**

Brigitte and Hank finish the main course.

*Waiter*: Would you like anything else?

*Hank*: Can we see the menu, please?

**(f) Dialogue 6**

Later.

*Waiter*: Can I give you a little more coffee?

*Brigitte*: No, thank you. Could you bring us the bill, please?

*Waiter*: Here it is.

*Brigitte*: Is service included?

*Waiter*: Yes, it is.

## 5.2 VOCABULARY

**(a) Dialogue 1**

  **(i) Useful expressions**
  - Come this way, please.
    Use this expression when you want someone to follow you.
  - Would you like to . . .
  - Could I have a . . .
    (see page 48 for explanation)

  **(ii) Words to learn**
  - beer
    An alcoholic drink made from hops. There are many different kinds of beer.
    Bitter and lager are types of beer.
  - a pint
    1 pint = 0.568 litre
    In Britain people often ask for: a pint of bitter (or lager) or half a pint of bitter.
  - menu
    A list of food you can eat or order.
    (there is a menu on page 45)

What's on the menu?
I'd like the menu of the day, please.
- hungry
  When you are hungry, you want to eat.
  I'm very hungry. My last meal was yesterday.
  A hungry child.

## (b) Dialogue 2

### (i) Useful expressions
I'll have the mushrooms
The mushrooms, the soup, *etc.* = a simple way of asking for food in a restaurant without repeating the name on the menu.

### (ii) Vocabulary
red meat
Meat such as beef or lamb which is dark brown after you cook it. Chicken is white meat.
I don't like red meat.

## (c) Dialogue 3

### (i) Useful expressions
- Are you ready to order?
  To order is to ask for something to be brought to you.
  Can you come and take our order? (to a waiter)
  I ordered some chicken.
- I'm all right
  A way of refusing an offer of more to drink.

### (ii) Words to learn
- roast
  To roast is to cook meat in an oven or over the fire.
  I ordered roast beef.
  We roasted a chicken for dinner.
- cream
  A white liquid taken from milk. You use cream to cook with or to put on fruit or desserts.
  In England, you can buy single cream, double cream (thicker) or clotted cream (very thick).
- medium
  A way of describing how red meat is cooked.
  Rare = cooked so the meat is still red
  Well done = cooked so there is no blood
  Medium = cooked in between
  How would you like it cooked? Rare, please.
  I like my meat well done.

**(d) Dialogue 4**
  (i) **Words to learn**
  • French fries
    Long, thin pieces of potato fried in oil or fat. Used in British and American English. In British English they are also called chips.
  • Fish and chips
    I had chicken and chips.
    In American English, chips or potato chips are hard, thin slices of fried potato. In British English, these are crisps.

**(e) Dialogues 5 & 6**
  (i) **Useful expressions**
    Would you like anything else?
    Polite question at the end of a meal.

  (ii) **Words to learn**
    bill

    service
    You get service in a shop
    or restaurant. In Britain
    10% to 15% is sometimes
    added to a bill for service.
    There is no service charge on the bill.
    Is a service charge included in the bill?
    The service in the hotel was very good.
    Could we have some service, please?

## 5.3 EXPLANATIONS

**(a) Little/a few**
A small amount or quantity.
Few is used with plural countable nouns, little is used with singular uncountable nouns.
In conversation we normally use a few and a little rather than few and little.

**(b) Would**
For offering and inviting, we use would you like . . .?
Would you like a beer?

*Note*: Do not use: Do you like . . .? It has a different meaning.
I'd like (I would like) is a polite way of saying what you want.

## (c) Can/could
We often use can or could to ask someone to do something.
Can you bring the menu, please?
Could you pass the salt, please?
Could you . . . is more polite than can you . . .
In England it is very important to say please when you ask for something.
We sometimes use can to make an offer.
Can I help you?
Can I get you a drink?

## (d) Will
We often use will ('ll) when we decide something at the moment we're speaking.
What would you like to eat? I'll have a steak, please.
I think I'll go to dinner.
We also use will to:
  (i) offer to do something.
      Will you bring us the bill, please?
 (ii) ask someone to do something.
      Will you bring us the bill, please?

## 5.4 BACKGROUND

### (a) Menus
  (i) **Breakfast 07:00 – 09:00**

The traditional English breakfast is fried eggs, bacon, toast, marmalade (jam made with oranges and sugar). People drink tea or coffee.

But many people have cereals with milk, or a boiled egg.

(ii) **Lunch 12:00 – 14:00**

For many people, lunch is a small meal. People have sandwiches, salads or pies.

The word dinner is also used when lunch is the main meal.

(iii) **Dinner 18:00 – 20:00**

For some, dinner is the main meal of the day. There may be a starter or first course, a main course and a pudding for desert. The menu on page 45 has some traditional English dishes.

Tea, supper and evening meal are also used for a lighter evening meal.

Most people do not have time for the traditional afternoon tea of sandwiches, cake, scones, cream, jam and tea at 17:00! Instead they have a lot of snacks.

## 5.5 EXERCISES

### Section A

### Exercise 1
Complete these dialogues.
A: Good evening, John. . . . . . . . I get you a drink?
B: Yes, I'll have . . . . . . . of bitter, please.

A: What would you . . . . . . . to eat?
B: I . . . . . . . I'll have the duck.

A: Waiter, . . . . . . . you bring us the bill, please.
B: Certainly, sir, would you like . . . . . . . more coffee?

### Exercise 2
Write a little or a few.
a  Would you like . . . . . . . cream in your soup?
b  Would you like more vegetables? I'll have . . . . . . . potatoes, please?
c  Are you hungry? There's . . . . . . . cheese on the table.
d  Can you please bring us . . . . . . . apples?
e  Would you like more wine? Just . . . . . . . .

52

*f* Shall we have . . . . . . . sandwiches for tea?
*g* I'd like . . . . . . . milk with my coffee, please.
*h* How many people are there in the restaurant? . . . . . . . .
*i* How much food is there? . . . . . . . .

**Exercise 3**
You are Brigitte or Hank. Use the menu on page 45 to complete the order as in the example.

*Waiter*:  What would you like for your main course?
*You*:  (Ask for the steak)
   I'd like the steak, please. or I'll have steak, please.

*Waiter*:  What would you like for dessert?
*You*:  (Ask for the pie)
*Waiter*:  Would you like cream with the pie?
*You*:  (Refuse the cream. Ask for ice-cream)
*Waiter*:  Certainly. Would you like coffee now or later?
*You*:  (Ask for it later)

**Section B**

**Exercise 4**
Countable or uncountable. Write C or U in the boxes.

| | | | |
|---|---|---|---|
| chips | ☐ | steak and kidney pie | ☐ |
| cheese | ☐ | prawn cocktail | ☐ |
| crisps | ☐ | beer | ☐ |
| beef | ☐ | glass of wine | ☐ |
| coffee | ☐ | apple | ☐ |

**Exercise 5**
Write what you would say in these situations. There is an example to help you.
You are at the hotel reception. You want to change a twenty dollar note. (Can you . . .?)
Can you change a twenty dollar note, please?
1 You are at the airport. Your bag is very heavy. Ask for help. (Can you . . .?)

   . . . . . . . . . . . . . . . . . . . . . . . . . . . . . . . . . . . . . . . . . . . . . . . . . . . . . . . . . . . . . . . . . . . . . .
2 You are at dinner. The salt is at the other end of the table. Ask someone to pass it. (Could you . . .?)

   . . . . . . . . . . . . . . . . . . . . . . . . . . . . . . . . . . . . . . . . . . . . . . . . . . . . . . . . . . . . . . . . . . . . . .

3 You want to find Trafalgar Square. You are lost. Ask someone.
(Could you . . .?)

4 You are in a restaurant. Ask the waiter for a glass of wine. (Could
you . . .?)

..................................................................................

5 You are in a shop. You want to try a red blouse. (Can I . . .?)

..................................................................................

6 You are in a restaurant. You want to pay. (Waiter, could I
have . . .?)

..................................................................................

7 You are at a hotel reception. You want to speak to a Mr. Brown.
(Could I . . .?)

..................................................................................

**Writing**
Look at the description of English food on page 50.
Write about the food in your country as in the example.
Breakfast 07:30
The traditional Turkish breakfast is white cheese, olives and
bread. People have tea . . .

# CHAPTER 6

# WHAT SORT OF THINGS

# DOES HE LIKE?

## 6.1 DIALOGUES

**(a) Dialogue 1**

Brigitte telephones her pen friend.

*Margaret:* 881 7436

*Brigitte:* Hello, could I speak to Margaret Ward, please?

*Margaret:* Speaking.

*Brigitte:* Margaret, this is Brigitte!

*Margaret:* Oh, hello! Where are you calling from?

*Brigitte:* I'm at the Balmoral Hotel in London.

*Margaret:* Look. I'm sorry I'm very busy now so I can't talk. Can we meet for a drink this evening?

*Brigitte:* Sure.

*Margaret:* Great. There's a pub I often go to in the same street as the Balmoral Hotel. It's called the 'Three Bells'. See you there at 8 p.m.

**(b) Dialogue 2**

At the pub.

*Margaret*: Brigitte! Over here.

*Brigitte*: Hello, Margaret. Good to see you.

*Margaret*: What can I get you?

*Brigitte*: I'd like a gin and tonic, please.

(A minute later)

*Margaret*: Here you are. Cheers. It's wonderful to see you in London. What's new?

*Brigitte*: Well, I have a surprise for you. I'm engaged.

*Margaret*: Congratulations. That's wonderful news. What's your fiancé's name?

*Brigitte*: His name's Hermann and he lives in Düsseldorf.

*Margaret*: Is he a student, too?

*Brigitte*: No, he works for a bank.

*Margaret*: How old is he?

*Brigitte*: He's twenty-three. I've got a photograph of him here.

*Margaret*: He's very nice. What sort of things does he like? Does he like music?

*Brigitte*: Oh, yes. He's very fond of music. He plays the violin for a small orchestra.

*Margaret*: And sport?

*Brigitte*: He likes football and tennis. We play tennis once a week. He's better than me but it's fun.

*Margaret*: And what languages does he speak?

*Brigitte*: Well, English, of course. A little French and Spanish too. That's all.

*Margaret*: He sounds really nice.

*Brigitte*:  He is. How's Andrew?
*Margaret*:  I don't see him any more. He doesn't really like the same things as I do, and I don't have the time with the new job.
*Brigitte*:  Oh yes, do you like it?
*Margaret*:  Very much. The hours are long. I work from . . .

## 6.2 VOCABULARY

### (a) Dialogue 1
#### (i) Useful expressions
● When you answer the telephone, you usually say:
the number, as Margaret did, or your name or the name of your business: **Margaret Ward, Balmoral Hotel**, or **Hello!**
Double eight = 88
Double two = 22
Oh = 0 when giving a telephone number. We also say **zero** or **nought**.
● Speaking = short for: This is Margaret speaking.
We often use it on the telephone, in reply to **Can I speak to** . . . . . . ., **please?**
*Andrew*:  Is John there, please?
*John*:  Speaking.
*Andrew*:  John, it's Andrew Black. Hi.
*Note*:  Don't use **yes** for speaking.

#### (ii) Words to learn
● To call
If you call someone, you telephone them.
*A*:  Can I speak to Margaret, please?
*B*:  Who's calling?
● A pub
A building where people have a drink (often alcohol) and talk to their friends.

### (b) Dialogue 2
#### (i) Useful expressions
● What can I get you?
Expression you use to offer someone a drink in a pub.
● Gin and tonic
Tonic is a soft drink that is often mixed with gin.
● Cheers!
Something people say before a drink of alcohol.

- I'm engaged
  If two people are engaged
  they agree to marry.
  Usually, the woman wears
  an engagement ring

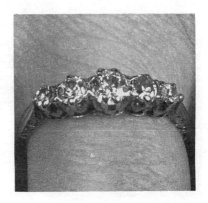

(ii) **Words to Learn**
  - Congratulations!
    Expression to show you are happy or pleased about something.
  - Fiancé
    A woman's fiancé is the man she is engaged to.
    A man's fiancée is the woman he is engaged to.
    Brigitte is Hermann's fiancée.
  - He's fond of
    To be fond of = like
    You can be fond of something or someone.
    I'm fond of beer.
    I'm fond of Margaret.
    You can also say
    I'm fond of playing tennis.
  - To play
    In English we use to play for:
    sports

They're playing cricket.

games

They're playing cards.

musical instruments

He's playing the violin.

Better
Comparative of good: good   better   best

## 6.3 EXPLANATIONS

### (a) The present simple
#### (i) Form

| Positive | Negative | Interrogative |
|---|---|---|
| I work | I don't work | Do I work? |
| he/she/it works | he/she/it doesn't work | Does he/she/it work? |
| you work | you don't work | Do you work? |
| we work | we don't work | Do we work? |
| you work | you don't work | Do you work? |
| they work | they don't work | Do they work? |

*Note*: The s in he works, she drinks, it lives, *etc*.

(ii) **Use**

The uses of the present simple include expressing:

- something that happens all the time or repeatedly
  I often go to the pub.
  She works at an advertising agency.
- how often we do things
  We play tennis once a week.
- something that is generally true.
  Water boils at 100 degrees centigrade.
- actions when we tell a story in the present tense.
  She walks in the pub. She buys a drink. She sits down

We also use the simple present for the present form of the verbs: to know, to like, to love, to hate, to understand, to think

We don't use: I am liking.

**(b) The present simple vs The present continuous**

Look at these examples.

| Present continuous | Present simple |
|---|---|
| Is Margaret speaking German? | Margaret speaks English. |
| He's working in a hotel for the summer. | He works for IBM in Germany. |

| Use the present continuous for something: | Use the present simple for something: |
|---|---|
| • which is happening at or around the time of speaking. | • general or which happens repeatedly. |
| • you see as temporary. | • you see as permanent. |

Laurent is living and studying in London. (This is temporary)
Laurent's family live in France. (Something that is permanent as far as we know)

## 6.4 BACKGROUND

**Pubs**

Pubs (short for public houses) are an important part of British life. Almost every town or village has a pub. In a pub you can relax, talk to people, play games like darts or bar billiards and have a drink as well. Pubs sell alcoholic and non-alcoholic drinks. Today more British people are drinking wine but beer is still the most popular

drink in a pub. In some pubs you can eat as well. Most pubs have more than one bar. The public bar is often more popular. The games and music are in the public bar.

The lounge bar (or saloon) is usually quieter and more comfortable. Children under 14 aren't allowed to go into bars which serve alcohol but some pubs have family rooms or gardens where children can drink non-alcoholic drinks.

People under 18 aren't permitted to buy or drink alcohol in pubs.

Most pubs open and close twice a day and there are opening and closing times which are called licensing hours.

In most pubs the landlord shouts: Last orders please! before the pub closes.

Go to the bar if you want another drink before the pub closes. When the landlord of a pub shouts: Time! you have 10 minutes to finish your drink.

## 6.5 EXERCISES

### Section A

### Exercise 1
Write down the phone numbers as in the example.
Double eight one five oh seven
8 8 1 5 0 7

1 ................................................................................................
   31 11 11

2 ................................................................................................
   0223 842315

3 ................................................................................................
   051 678 1626

4 ................................................................................................
   242036

**Exercise 2**
Write the correct form of the verb.
Brigitte (live) in Düsseldorf.
Brigitte **lives** in Düsseldorf.
Brigitte and Hermann (to be) engaged. They (to live) in Düsseldorf.
Brigitte (to be) a student but Hermann (to work) for a bank. Every week, they (to play) tennis together. Hermann also (to play) the violin in an orchestra. Both Hermann and Brigitte (to speak) good English.

**Exercise 3**
Write the correct form of the negative.
Margaret (not have) a fiancé.
Margaret **doesn't have** a fiancé.
1 Brigitte (not work) for a bank.
2 Margaret (not go) to the museum very often.
3 Brigitte and Hermann (not play) tennis twice a week.
4 I (not have) time to go.
5 Margaret (not speak) Spanish or French.
6 Hermann (not live) in Berlin.
7 Margaret (not see) Andrew any more.
8 The Scherers (not speak) English at home.

**Exercise 4**
Use these sentences to make questions. Begin the question with the word in brackets.
Brigitte studies. (Where)
**Where does Brigitte study?**
1 Hermann plays the violin. (Does?)
2 Margaret works. (Where?)
3 Margaret goes to 'The Three Bells'. (How often?)
4 I like music. (Do?)
5 I start work in the morning. (What time?)
6 They go to the pub. (Why?)

## Section B

### Exercise 5
Decide whether the underlined verbs in the sentences are right or wrong. Correct those that are wrong.
I <u>don't like</u> beer. Right
Please be quiet! I <u>watch</u> television. Wrong: am watching

1 I'<u>m usually playing</u> football every Saturday.
2 <u>Do</u> you know the name of the author?
3 He's <u>understanding</u> German and French.
4 Look! Margaret's <u>speaking</u> French!
5 I'<u>m thinking</u> that the answer is wrong.
6 It's a bad year, prices <u>are rising</u> in all the shops.
7 I'm sorry I can't speak to you now. I <u>study</u> for my exam.
8 In England, the sun <u>sets</u> early in the winter.

### Exercise 6
Make questions to find out as much as you can about a person's day, interests, *etc.*
Here are some examples:
What time do you get up?
What sort of food do you like?

### Writing
This is Margaret's first letter to Brigitte. Write a similar letter about yourself.

16 Park Road
London SW18 2DJ

Dear Brigitte,

My name is Margaret Ward and I'm writing in response to your advertisement for a pen pal. I'm 16 years old and I'm a student in London. My father is a teacher and my mother is a doctor. I haven't got any brothers or sisters.

I'm fond of swimming and tennis and I play for my school team. In school my favourite subjects are English and Mathematics. I also like to read and listen to music. Do you?

I have two more years in school. My ambition is to go into business. What about you? I'm enclosing a photograph of myself at the school dance. I want to write to someone in Germany so please reply soon.

I look forward to hearing from you.
Yours sincerely
Margaret Ward

# CHAPTER 7

# NOBODY UNDERSTOOD ME

## 7.1 DIALOGUES 📼

**(a) Dialogue 1**

Brigitte and Margaret are in the pub.

*Margaret*:  I don't know . . .

*Brigitte*:  Just a minute. There's a friend of mine over there. Laurent, Laurent . . .

*Laurent*:  Oh, hello, Brigitte. I didn't see you. What are you doing here?

*Brigitte*:  I'm having a drink with my friend, Margaret. Margaret, this is Laurent. Laurent's studying English in London at the moment.

*Margaret*:  Pleased to meet you.

*Brigitte*:  Look, are you waiting for someone? Why don't you join us?

*Laurent*:  Sure.

*Brigitte*:  Well, did you have a good day, Laurent?

*Laurent*:  Not bad, but I got lost this morning.

*Brigitte*:  How?

*Laurent*:  Well, I got up, had breakfast and went to the tube station as usual but the station was closed, so I decided to take a taxi. I waited and waited and as there were no taxis around I started to walk but I got lost . . .

*Brigitte*:  Oh no. What did you do?

*Laurent*:  Well, I tried to ask the way but everyone I met was a foreigner. It was terrible. Nobody understood me.

*Brigitte*:  So what happened?

*Laurent*:  I walked round and round until suddenly I saw a sign for the Haymarket. The school is not far from there so I followed the sign and arrived just over an hour late.

**(b) Dialogue 2**

The conversation continues.

*Laurent*: So, what did you do today?

*Brigitte*: After I telephoned Margaret this morning I went for a walk round Central London. I visited the National Gallery in the morning. Then I had lunch in Chinatown and in the afternoon I walked round Covent Garden.

*Margaret*: Did you buy anything?

*Brigitte:* No, I was just window-shopping. The small boutiques and shops in Covent Garden are quite expensive. How about you, Margaret? How was your day?

*Margaret*: Busy! We had a presentation for a new client this afternoon so there was a lot to do and organise. I'm glad it's over. Anyway it's really good to see you here.

## 7.2 VOCABULARY

**(a) Dialogue 1**

   (i) **Useful expressions**

   - to have a drink with someone

     If you have a meal or a drink, it means you eat or drink something.

     To have a meal or drink with someone is to do it in company.

     So, to have lunch is to eat lunch. (see Dialogue 2)

   - Come and have a meal with me next Saturday.
   - To get lost

     To lose your way so that you don't know which way to go.

   - How?
   - What did you do then?
   - What happened?

     Use these expressions with a slight rise in intonation to get a person to continue telling a story.

**(b) Dialogue 2**

   (i) **Words to Learn**

   - a presentation

     When you present a product to a client you give them information about it.

   - window-shopping

     When you window-shop, you look at shops without buying anything.

## 7.3 EXPLANATIONS

### (a) The past simple
The past simple is used to talk about actions or situations in the past. It is sometimes called the story-telling tense.

### Form
Past simple verbs often end in -ed.
The positive of the regular verbs is the base of the verb with -ed.
rain   rained
There are four basic spellings of the regular form.
1 -ed
   work worked   play played   happen happened   wait waited
2 -d (use with verbs ending with a silent e)
   live lived   arrive arrived
3 -(p)ed (use with consonants + vowel + consonant)
   stop stopped
4 -ied (in words with a consonant + y)
   carry carried   study studied
However, many important verbs are irregular.
   buy bought   understand understood
There is a list of the main irregular verbs on page 268.
The negative and interrogative forms of the regular and irregular verbs are the same.

| Positive | Negative | Interrogative |
|----------|----------|---------------|
| She worked<br>She understood | She did not work<br>She did not understand | Did she work?<br>Did she understand? |

The past of the verb **to be** is **was/were**.
I/She/He/It **was**   we/you/they **were**

## 7.4 BACKGROUND

### (a) London
A gallery is a place that has works of art on exhibition. The National Gallery in Trafalgar Square is one of London's best known art galleries.

Chinatown is an area of central London where there are a lot of Chinese restaurants, supermarkets, businesses, *etc.*

Covent Garden is an area of shops and restaurants built in and around the old fruit and vegetable market made famous in Shaw's 'Pygmalion' and the musical, 'My Fair Lady'.

Covent Garden is also the name used for The Royal Opera House in the same area.

### (b) Shops and shopping areas

Boutiques are small shops that sell fashionable clothes or jewellery and Covent Garden is full of them. In a large town many people shop at department stores. These are called department stores because there are departments or sections which sell almost everything, from beds and kitchen equipment to clothing and perfume, and you can buy most things in one place. Two famous London department stores are Selfridge's and Harrod's.

Many people buy a lot of basic items like underwear and sweaters from chain stores like Marks and Spencer's. Other well-known chains sell shoes, clothing, household goods, *etc.* and many British High Streets have shops in national chains.

Many towns have shopping centres which contain many different shops. Some of the more recent shopping centres are good places to shop because they are covered and are comfortable places to walk round in the summer or the winter.

Many British towns still have traditional market stalls which sell food and vegetables as well as cheap clothing, records, *etc.* Some markets are also famous for second-hand goods and antiques.

Despite attractive markets most people buy food from super-markets, where the shelves are full of food from many countries.

Napoleon said 'The English are a nation of shopkeepers'. Many towns and villages still have corner shops (which sell groceries and food), newsagents' (newspapers and tobacco) and chemists' (medecine) but the small shop is gradually disappearing from the towns as more chains appear in what some people call 'The High Street revolution'.

## 7.5 **EXERCISES**

### Section A

### Exercise 1
Match these present and past forms of irregular verbs.

| Present | Past |
| --- | --- |
| go | left |
| wake | ate |
| sleep | had |
| see | said |
| leave | could |
| tell | went |
| stand | told |
| eat | stood |
| can | woke |
| have | saw |
| say | slept |

**Exercise 2**
Here is a list of things Brigitte had to do today. She didn't have time
to do all of them. Which ones did she do? Which ones didn't she do?
**She telephoned Margaret.**
**She didn't write a postcard home.**
telephone Margaret ✓
write a postcard home
visit the National Portrait Gallery ✓
go round Covent Garden ✓
buy a present for her mum
change money
meet Hank for dinner
go to the theatre

**Exercise 3**
Complete the following questions using verbs from the box.

| see   meet   telephone   go   have |

1 . . . . . . Brigitte . . . . . . . shopping yesterday?
   Yes, she did.
2 Who . . . . . . she . . . . . . in the morning?
   Margaret.
3 What time . . . . . . she . . . . . . Margaret in the pub?
   At 8.00 p.m.
4 Who . . . . . . they . . . . . . in the pub?
   They saw Laurent.
5 What . . . . . . she . . . . . . to drink?
   A gin and tonic.

**Section B**

**Exercise 4**
Margaret is asking Brigitte about her first few days in London. Make
up her questions.
when/arrive?    When did you arrive?
plane/late?     Was the plane late?


1 how many suitcases/have?    .................................................
2 which airport/arrive at?    .................................................
3 how/travel to London?    .................................................
4 how much/taxi cost?    .................................................

5 what/weather like? .......................................................
6 what/name of the hotel? ..............................................
7 have/reservation? ......................................................
8 what time/arrive at the hotel? .......................................
Look back at Chapters 1 & 2 and give Brigitte's answers.

**Exercise 5**
Margaret is describing the start of a recent holiday.
Put the verbs in brackets in the past tense.
I . . . . . . (to leave) home at about 5.30 p.m. I . . . . . . . (to be)
very sleepy but the roads . . . . . . (to be) empty and I . . . . . . (to
arrive) in Dover in 1½ hours. I . . . . . . . (to catch) the 7.30 ferry to
Calais. The journey . . . . . . (to take) just over an hour and I
. . . . . . (to sleep) for most of it. It . . . . . . . (to take) me about
half an hour to find my way out of Calais. I . . . . . . (to stop) for
breakfast in a café just outside Calais before I . . . . . . (to start) the
long drive to meet my friend in Lyon.

**Writing**
You are Laurent. Describe what happened to you in Dialogue 1.
Compare what you wrote with the version on page 216.

# CHAPTER 8

# WHERE SHALL WE GO?

## 8.1 DIALOGUES 📼

**(a) Dialogue 1**

Brigitte, Laurent and Margaret are still in the pub.

*Laurent*: Look, it's late. I have to go.

*Brigitte*: Right, Laurent. See you!

*Margaret*: Gosh, is it already half past ten? Look, what are you doing for the rest of the week?

*Brigitte*: Well, I'm going to Cambridge on Thursday.

*Margaret*: Right, why don't you meet my cousin, Peter. He'll be pleased to show you round. He's at the University but he's on holiday at the moment. I'll give him a ring to see if he'll be free.

*Brigitte:* That's very kind. I'm taking the 9 o'clock train from London. Are you sure it won't be too much trouble?

*Margaret*: Not at all. Let's see, I'm going to be very busy for the rest of the week. I'm in Birmingham on Wednesday and Thursday so I won't be able to see you but let's go away for the weekend.

*Brigitte*: I haven't got any plans yet. Where shall we go?

*Margaret*: I know. How about going to visit my grandmother in Yorkshire? She's got a small cottage and there are a lot of places we can visit near there. We'll go for walks. It'll be great fun. What do you think?

*Brigitte*: Are you sure she won't mind?

*Margaret*: No. She loves visitors. Look, I'll telephone you tomorrow evening to let you know about Cambridge and arrange to meet you to go to Leeds on Saturday morning. Shall we go now? I'll walk with you back to your hotel.

**(b) Dialogue 2**

Next morning Brigitte sees Hank in the hotel after breakfast.

*Hank*: Hi! What are your plans for the day?

*Brigitte*: I'm going to visit the British Museum.

*Hank*: Hey, look at those huge black clouds. It's going to rain. Can I come with you?

*Brigitte*: Why not? I'll just go up to my room to get my coat and umbrella. I think I'll need it!

*Hank*: Fine, I'll see you down here in about five minutes.

## 8.2 VOCABULARY

**(a) Dialogue 1**

(i) **Useful expressions**

- See you!

  Informal way of saying goodbye.

  We also say See you later or Be seeing you.

- to give someone a ring

  to telephone someone

- trouble

  to have trouble doing something is to have difficulties or problems.

  Did you have any trouble finding our house?

  Will it cause trouble?

  Are you sure it won't be any trouble?

- Not at all

  A strong way of saying no.

- Why don't you?

  Why + not is a suggestion in the form of a question.

  Why not ring her now?

  Why don't you sit down, you look tired?

- to be delighted

  to be very happy

  he'll be free

  he won't be working or have anything to do.

  I work on Saturday but I'm free on Tuesdays.

  How about?

  Informal offer or suggestion.

  How about going to the cinema?

  How about is followed by the -ing form.

  We also use How would you like to . . .?

- Let's . . .
  Informal suggestion
  Let's go out to dinner.
- I haven't got any plans yet.
  In a negative statement like this, yet means up to the moment of speaking. So, Brigitte has no plans.
- mind
  Expressions like do you mind are a polite way of asking permission.
  She won't mind = She will not be unhappy or will have no objection.
- to go for a walk
  Usually a walk for pleasure.
  We'll go for a walk in the park.

(ii) **Words to learn**
- grandmother
  mother of your father or mother
- cousin
  child of your uncle or aunt (*i.e* child of the brother or sister of your mother or father)
- weekend
  In England the weekend is usually Saturday and Sunday. Sometimes Friday evening is part of the weekend.
- plans
  If you have plans, you intend to do something.
  What are your plans for the weekend?
  I haven't got any plans for my summer holiday yet.
- cottage
  a small house

## 8.3 EXPLANATIONS

### (a) The present continuous future
We use the present continuous future when we are talking about arrangements we have decided on.
Brigitte is going to Cambridge on Tuesday.
Brigitte and Margaret are spending the weekend in Yorkshire.

### (b) The 'going to' future
We use going to (do) something when we have decided what to do in the future. This is very similar to the present continuous future. So, we can say I'm flying to Paris next week or I'm going to fly to Paris next week.

We also use **going to** to say what we think will happen in the near future. Usually, something in the present leads us to make the statement. For example black clouds lead Hank to say:
It's going to rain.

#### (c) The shall/will future
We often use **will** to predict something in the future. Often we use the expressions **I think** or **I'm sure** as well.
I am sure he'll be free.
I'll probably go alone.

(i) **Form**
In spoken English we normally use the short forms **I'll, we'll.**
The negative of **will** is **will not** or **won't.**
The negative of **shall** is **shall not** or **shan't.**
We use **will** for strong intention so we say:
Will you take this man to be your husband?
I will (not I shall).
The form **Shall we** . . . is often used for offers and suggestions.
We don't use **will we** . . .

(ii) **I'll do it tomorrow vs. I'm going to do it tommorow.**
We use **I'll** . . . when we decide something at the moment of speaking (see Chapter 5) When we use **I'm going to** . . . we have already made the plan or arrangement.
*A:* Can you clean the car, please?
*B:* OK! I'll do it this afternoon.
*A:* Can you clean the car, please? I don't want to tell you again!
*B:* Don't worry. I'm going to clean it this afternoon.

#### (d) Any
We use **any** with uncountable and plural nouns in negative and interrogative sentences. It has the same kind of meaning as **a/an.**
I haven't got any plans.
Have you got any plans?

### 8.4 BACKGROUND

#### The pleasures of life – English style
Going away for the weekend is a pleasure of life for some. It is a chance to get away from home to visit friends or stay at one of the many pubs or hotels which advertise weekend breaks with walking, golf, *etc.*

But what do people do in their spare time?

Well, they watch quite a lot of television (over 20 hours per week) and although the British have a reputation for sports, only 5% of the population take part in organised sport.

Away from the home, some 50% of people go to the pub. Today leisure is based around the home. Records, tapes, and books are very popular but two very British activities are gardening and D-I-Y which stands for Do-it-yourself.

The most popular activity that people take part in is walking. Going for a walk (often with a dog) gives exercise and pleasure to many. Other popular sports that people take part in are indoor activities such as billiards and snooker, darts and swimming.

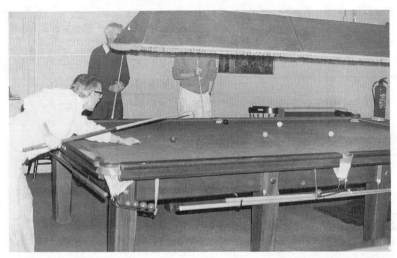

The most popular spectator sport on television is snooker but many watch football, athletics and rugby. Cricket is still a popular spectator sport during international matches, which are called test matches, but games new to Britain such as American Football are becoming popular with younger people.

## 8.5 EXERCISES

**Section A**

**Exercise 1**
Make sentences about Brigitte's plans for the rest of the week from
this information in her diary.

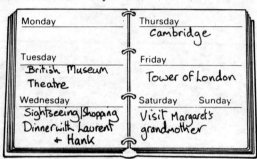

On Tuesday, she's going to the British Museum.
She's visiting the British Museum on Tuesday.

**Exercise 2**
Put the verb in the correct form using will or going to.
*Margaret*:   Where are you going on Tuesday?
*Brigitte*:   I'm going (go) to Cambridge

*Brigitte*:   Oh no! I haven't got his address.
*Margaret*:   I'll telephone (telephone) him and ask this evening.

1 *Brigitte*:   Did you remember to buy me a newspaper.
  *Laurent*:   I'm terribly sorry I forgot. I . . . . . . . (get) you one
       later.
2 *Hank*:   What are you doing this evening?
  *Brigitte*:   I . . . . . . . (meet) my friend Margaret at the pub.
3 *Brigitte*:   Oh look! It's raining.
  *Hank*:   Don't worry! I . . . . . . . (go) and get us an umbrella.
4 *Laurent:*   What would you like to drink, beer or wine?
  *Hank*:   I . . . . . . . (have) a glass of wine, please.
5 *Brigitte*:   If you wait a moment . . . . . . . (go) and get my coat
       from my room.
  *Hank*:   I . . . . . . . (be) right here.
6 *Laurent*:   So Margaret . . . . . . . (be) in Birmingham next
       week. Shall we go to the cinema?
  *Brigitte*:   I . . . . . . . (think) about it.

**Exercise 3**

Use **Shall I . . .** or **Shall we . . .** in each of these situations.

Hank and Brigitte are in the hotel lounge. It is very hot but the window is closed. Hank says . . . **Shall I open the window?**

1 Laurent and Brigitte are in the hotel restaurant. It is late. Brigitte is tired and the restaurant is closing. She says . . . . . . . .

2 Brigitte and Margaret are looking at a newspaper. They want to go somewhere this evening. Margaret sees an advertisement for a film. She says . . . . . . . .

3 It's Laurent's birthday. She wants to buy him a present. She asks Hank for a suggestion and says What . . . . . . .

4 Laurent and Brigitte are having tea together. Laurent picks up the tea pot and says . . . . . . .

5 Brigitte and Margaret are in a restaurant. They have the menu. Brigitte sees a dish for two. She wants to try it. She asks . . . . . . .

**Section B**

**Exercise 4**

Make an appropriate suggestion or offer for each situation.

You are with some friends. The food is ready.

(Let's) . . . **Let's eat**

1 You are with your partner at a dance. The music starts.
   (Shall we) ....................................................................

2 You are with some friends. You are all hungry.
   (How about) ....................................................................

3 You notice a friend is feeling cold. His/her coat is on the chair.
   (Shall I) ....................................................................

4 You have nothing to do. You decide to invite a friend to the cinema.
   (Would you) ....................................................................

5 Your friend is having trouble painting a door. You want to do it for him.
   (Let me) ....................................................................

**Exercise 5**

Here are some predictions about life in the future.

1 People will decide on the IQ, sex, height, *etc.* of their babies in advance.

2 All shopping will be done from home using a catalogue and a computer.

3 Nobody will have to work.

4 Robots will do all the routine jobs in the home.
5 Everyone will have an ideal weight through pills and diet food.
   Which predictions do you agree with?
   Which predictions do you disagree with?
   Change any predictions you disagree with.
Use sentences like
I agree that people will . . .
I don't think people will . . .
I think people will . . .
Now write 5 predictions of your own.

**Exercise 6**
You are interviewing the author of a book entitled 'Our future.'
Make up some questions to ask her.
live/cities   Will we live in cities?
1  people live/longer
2  have/nuclear weapons
3  America be/the richest nation
4  children speak/one language
Make some more questions of your own using what, when, how *etc.*

**Writing**
You have two free tickets to the Arts Theatre next weekend.
Write a short note inviting a friend to come with you.
Find out what he/she is doing.
Suggest he/she comes with you to the theatre.
Suggest a place to meet.
Ask him/her to telephone you to confirm the meeting.
Compare your note with the one on page 217.

# WE COULD SEE THE

# PHANTOM OF

# THE OPERA

## 9.1 DIALOGUES 📼

### (a) Dialogue 1

Hank and Brigitte return to the hotel after visiting the British Museum.

*Hank*: Gee, that was fun. I really enjoyed the Egyptian room with all those mummies. Weren't they terrific?

*Brigitte*: Yes, it was very interesting. Look, I'm rather tired so I think I'll go to my room and have a bath.

*Hank*: Sure. Say Brigitte, Laurent and I are thinking of going to the theatre tonight. Do you think you might be interested?

*Brigitte*: I might. What are you going to see?

*Hank*: I don't know yet . . . Well, go and have your bath and see us in the bar at about 7 p.m.

### (b) Dialogue 2

Laurent and Hank are in the bar.

*Hank*: Well, Laurent. What do you think? Where shall we go?

*Laurent*: We could go and see 'The Phantom of the Opera'.

*Hank*: I don't think we'll be able to get tickets. It's booked up till the new year.

*Laurent*: Well, we could try and see if there are any returns.

*Hank*: There's always a long queue, and if there aren't any tickets, it'll be too late to see another show.

*Laurent*: So what would you suggest?

*Hank*: Well, we could go and see a play. There's a new version of 'Twelfth Night' at the National Theatre. What do you think?

*Laurent*: Well, I find Shakespeare very difficult to follow.

*Hank*: Well, this one's a comedy, and there's a lot of action.

*Laurent*: Look, here's Brigitte. You can ask her.

**(c) Dialogue 3**

Brigitte arrives at the bar.

*Brigitte*: Good evening, gentlemen. Well, what are we going to see?

*Hank*: We're trying to decide. Would you prefer the musical 'The Phantom of the Opera' or a play by Shakespeare?

*Brigitte*: I think the musical would suit me better.

*Hank*: All right. If there are tickets for 'The Phantom of the Opera' we'll go and see it. But what shall we do if we don't get in?

*Laurent*: Well, we could go to the cinema instead. What do you think?

*Brigitte*: Are there any good films on at the moment?

*Laurent*: Lots. Look!

*Hank*: Right, that's settled then. We'll try to get into the Phàntom and if we can't, we'll go and see a film. Shall we go and get a snack before the show? We could go for supper afterwards but I need something now.

*Brigitte*: What a good idea! I'm starving.

*Laurent:* Er Look, I'm not hungry, so I'll go to the theatre to start queueing.

*Hank:* Fine. We might get in! See you later.

## 9.2 VOCABULARY

### (a) Dialogue 1

#### (i) Useful expressions

- Gee, that was fun!

  Gee! or Gee whiz! are informal expressions in American English. They are used to express a strong reaction.

  Gee, that was sad.

- Weren't they terrific?

  You use terrific when you are very pleased with something.

  I have a new job.

  That's terrific!

  Hank wants Brigitte to agree that the Egyptian room was wonderful.

- I'm rather tired

  Here rather is used to emphasise that Brigitte is tired.

- To go to the theatre

  To go to see a play or a show. Spelt theater in American English.

- Do you think you might . . .?

  A very polite way of asking.

#### (ii) Words to learn

- mummies

  Plural of mummy.

  Here it is a preserved body.

- But, mummy or mum are informal forms of mother.

  daddy or dad are informal forms of father.

  Where does your mum live?

### (b) Dialogue 2

#### (i) Useful expressions

- We could . . .

  When you use we could you mean that something is possible for you and the person(s) you are talking about.

  We could go next week.

- booked up

  If a restaurant or theatre is booked up it has no available seats.

  We also use fully booked.

- difficult to follow

  If you follow a story or play it means you understand it. If something is difficult to follow it is difficult to understand. The opposite is easy to follow.

### (ii) Words to learn

- returns

  When a theatre is fully booked, they sometimes sell tickets which people do not want any more just before a show. These are returns.

- a comedy

  A play or film that aims to make you laugh.

## (c) Dialogue 3

### (i) Useful expressions

- Would you prefer . . .?

  If you prefer something or someone, you like that thing or person more than another. So when there is a choice you can ask Would you prefer . . .?

  Would you prefer tea or coffee?

- That's settled

  That's decided.

- I'm starving

  To starve means to die from hunger. I'm starving means I'm very very hungry.

### (ii) Words to learn

- Cinema

  A cinema is a place where people go to watch films.

  Let's go to the cinema.

  What's showing at the Rex Cinema?

- Musical

  A play or film that uses singing and dancing as part of the story.

  'My Fair Lady' is a famous musical set in Covent Garden.

- snack

  A light quick meal. Sometimes it is eaten instead of a main meal. Sometimes it is eaten between meals.

  The flight from London to Paris takes about an hour so we only had a snack.

  Apple and cheese make a healthy snack.

- supper

  Here supper is a small meal you eat late at night. For example, after the theatre some people go out for supper.

  Supper can also mean an early evening meal. Usually informal.

  We went out for supper after the concert.

  Come to supper with the family at around 7 p.m.

## 9.3 EXPLANATIONS

### (a) May and Might
We use may or might to show that something is possible.
The meaning of the two is very similar.
He may be in the hotel (Perhaps he is in the hotel . . .) or
He might be in the hotel have almost the same meaning.
Where is he? He may be at home.
If they can't get tickets for the play they might go to the cinema.
We may go to Spain in July.

### (b) Could (do)
Could can be the past tense of can
However, we often use could to talk about possible future actions, especially when we make suggestions.
What shall we do this weekend? I know, we could stay with my aunt.
You could stay with us if you like.
can may be used in these examples as well, but it is more definite than could.

### (c) If + future
This is used for a real possibility that something will happen. We usually use the present tense to refer to the future in the 'if clause', not will or shall.
*If I will go to the office, I will wait for him is a common mistake. We should say:
If I go to the office, I will wait for him.

## 9.4 BACKGROUND

### West End theatreland
The West End is an area of Central London that includes the shopping areas of Oxford Street, Regent Street and Bond Street as well as the entertainment centres of Soho, Piccadilly Circus, Leicester Square and Shaftesbury Avenue.

The statue of Eros in Piccadilly Circus is near Soho. Soho was famous for bars and strip clubs but today there are many stylish shops and restaurants as well as a Chinatown. Today, Soho or Covent Garden, which is near by, are the places to go for a meal before or after a show. There are over 30 theatres in this small area known as the golden mile. There is something for every taste; musicals, comedies and thrillers as well as serious drama.

The heart of London's West End

Productions are advertised in the newspaper and you can buy tickets
from the theatre box-office or ticket agencies. As well as theatres, the
West End also has many of London's Cinemas.

For many visitors, London's theatre is a major attraction so make sure you book early!

## 9.5 EXERCISES

### Section A

### Exercise 1

Complete these sentences with the verb in the correct form.
If you go (go) for a snack, I will wait (wait) in the queue.
1 We could go to a musical, if we . . . . . . . (can get) tickets.
2 If we . . . . . . (not get in) to a musical, we . . . . . . (see) a film.

3 Why don't we go out?

I . . . . . . (come) if you . . . . . . (let) me buy the tickets.

4 If he . . . . . . (wait) to see me, . . . . . . (tell) him to go away.

5 If . . . . . . I (come) to London next week, I . . . . . . (give) you a ring.

6 I . . . . . . (be) at home, if you . . . . . . (come) before 8 p.m..

7 My mother and father . . . . . . (meet) you at the station if you . . . . . . (arrive) by train.

8 If you . . . . . . (pay) for dinner, I . . . . . . (pay) for the tickets.

## Exercise 2

Hank is talking to Laurent and Brigitte. Use might or might not to complete sentences about the things Hank is worried about.

It is difficult to get seats for 'The Phantom of the Opera'. Will they get any?

**We might not get seats . . .**

1 If there are no tickets for The Phantom, will they be too late for the other shows?

We ................................................................................

2 Hank is hungry. The show starts in five minutes. Will he have time to eat?

I ................................................................................

3 The tickets are very expensive. Will he have enough money?

I ................................................................................

4 The theatre is a long way away. There are no taxis. Will they be late?

We ................................................................................

5 The play is by Shakespeare. Will Laurent understand?

You ................................................................................

## Section B

## Exercise 3

Brigitte wants to go on holiday. She is not sure where she wants to go. Make some suggestions as to where she could go and what she could see.

India   **You could go to India and see the Taj Mahal.**

| | | |
|---|---|---|
| 1 New York | 5 | Pisa |
| 2 Paris | 6 | London |
| 3 Cairo | 7 | Sydney |
| 4 Athens | 8 | China |

**Exercise 4**

You live in London. Look at the map of London on page 27 and suggest places to go for different visitors.

Someone who likes Chinese food.

You could go to Soho.

Why don't you go to Chinatown.

1 Someone who likes shopping.

.....................................................................................................

2 Someone who is interested in Egyptian antiquities.

.....................................................................................................

3 Someone who likes the theatre.

.....................................................................................................

4 Someone who is interested in stock markets.

.....................................................................................................

5 Someone who wants to see the Queen.

.....................................................................................................

6 Someone who wants to wander round boutiques.

.....................................................................................................

7 Someone who wants to see Eros.

.....................................................................................................

**Exercise 5**

A visitor arrives in your town.

He/she does not have much time.

Suggest some places he/she might go to.

For example, in Madrid we might say

If you're interested in art, then you could go to the Prado.

If you want to go shopping try 'El Corte Ingles'; it's a big department store.

**Writing**

Write a short note to a friend.

1 Start with an appropriate greeting

   Dear . . . . . . .

2 Find out if they are free next weekend.

   What are you doing . . . . . . .

3 Suggest an activity.

   If you're free, why don't we . . . . . . .

4 Suggest a time and place to meet.

   We could meet . . . . . . .

5 Offer an alternative.

   If you can't . . . . . . .

6 Close

   Look forward to seeing you . . . . . . .

# AS I WAS WALKING DOWN OXFORD STREET

## 10.1 DIALOGUES 📼

### (a) Dialogue 1

The telephone rings at the reception of the Balmoral Hotel.

*Receptionist:* Good evening. Balmoral Hotel.

*Margaret:* Good evening. Could I have room 205, please?

*Receptionist:* Hold the line, please.
Erm, Miss Scherer isn't in her room. Would you like to leave a message?

*Margaret:* Please tell her that Margaret rang and she'll try again in half an hour.

*Receptionist:* Right, I'll make sure she gets the message.

*Margaret:* Thank you.

A little later, Brigitte arrives at reception.

*Receptionist:* Ah, good evening, Miss Scherer. You just missed a phone call. Someone called Margaret.

*Brigitte:* Oh dear. Did she leave a number?

*Receptionist:* No, but she'll call again in half an hour.

*Brigitte:* Thanks, I'll be in my room.

### (b) Dialogue 2

Margaret gets through to Brigitte.

*Margaret:* Hello! Where were you when I called earlier?

*Brigitte:* I was probably coming home on the tube. I'm sorry I wasn't here but I was delayed by something in Oxford Street.

*Margaret:* What happened?

*Brigitte:* Well, I was walking slowly down Oxford Street when I stopped to look in the window of a large store, and inside I

saw a woman who was putting some perfume straight from the shelf into her bag.

*Margaret*: What was she like?

*Brigitte*: She had red hair and was wearing a black coat and was very large, or seemed to be very large.

*Margaret*: What did you do?

*Brigitte*: I went in the shop but there were so many people that I couldn't see her. So, I left and continued window shopping, but when I walked into Selfridges, there she was again.

*Margaret*: What was she doing this time?

*Brigitte*: Well, she was looking at some sweaters in the fashion department and holding them up to try . . .. Well, she was doing this with her left hand and the next minute she just grabbed a sweater from the pile with her other hand and put it into her coat incredibly quickly . . ..I couldn't believe it . . ..This time, I went straight to the manager.

*Margaret*: Did they catch her?

*Brigitte*: Oh, yes. They followed her round and a security man stopped her as she was leaving the shop. Do you know, she wasn't really fat at all. It was all the things she had in the special inside pockets of her coat. The strange thing is that she was carrying a lot of money.

*Margaret*: Yes, shoplifting is a very big problem in the big London stores and strangely enough many shoplifters do have quite a lot of money on them when they're caught. Anyway, well done!

*Brigitte*: I suppose you're right! It just took so long.

*Margaret:* Look, I telephoned my grandmother this morning and she is looking forward to seeing us on Saturday. Shall I come to the hotel at around 9?

*Brigitte:* Are you sure it wouldn't be too much bother? I could meet you at the station.

*Margaret:* No, not at all. Look, why don't you . . .

## 10.2 VOCABULARY

### (a) Dialogue 1

#### (i) Useful expressions

- Good evening. Balmoral Hotel
  A way of answering the telephone if you are in a business.
  Greeting + name of business
  Good morning. European Airlines.

- Hold the line, please
  This means wait until the person you telephoned is available.

- I'm sorry, the line's engaged. Will you hold?
  Can you hold?

- Oh, dear!
  A mild expression to show you are sad, disappointed or surprised about something.
  Here, Brigitte is disappointed.
  *A:* I lost my ring last night.
  *B:* Oh, dear!

#### (ii) Words to learn

- to miss (something)
  To arrive too late for something
  You missed seeing him. (He left earlier before you arrived.)
  I missed the 07:00 train. I didn't arrive at the station till 07:05.

- message
  Information you leave when you cannot speak to someone directly.
  *A:* I'm sorry he isn't in.   *B:* Have you got a message?

### (b) Dialogue 2

#### (i) Useful expressions

- What was she like?
  A question asking about the woman's appearance.
  Some examples of like used to talk about appearance.
  They look like brothers.   She is like her sister.

- Well done!
  Expression to show that you are pleased about someone's action.
  *A:* I passed my exam. *B:* Well done!
  *A:* Right, I fixed your car. *B:* Well done!
- I suppose
  Here I suppose means Brigitte wants to agree with Margaret but she is really not sure.
- bother
  trouble or difficulty
  So, Brigitte does not want to give Margaret any trouble.
  I found your house without any bother.
  I'll do it for you. It won't be any bother.

(ii) **Words to learn**
- delayed
  If something delays you, it causes you to slow down or be late.
  I'm sorry I'm late. I was delayed by heavy traffic.
  The flight was delayed because of bad weather.
- perfume
  Chanel No. 5, Poison by Christian Dior, *etc,* are all perfumes
- store
  In this dialogue it is very large shop, short for department store
  In American English, store = shop
  She went to the store to buy some paper.
  In British English we also use store but usually when we say what kind of store it is.
  There are quite a few health-food stores in Cambridge.
  He has a small grocery store on the High street.
- to seem to be
  To give the appearance of being.
  He seems a lot older. (He is 30 but he looks 45)
- window shopping
  Looking at things in shops without buying anything.
  'What did you buy?' 'Nothing. I was just window shopping.'
- incredibly
  Adverb. If something is incredible it is difficult to believe.
- to grab
  To take something quickly.
  The thief grabbed her handbag.
  I grabbed a sandwich for lunch.

- shoplifting
  To steal something from a shop by putting it in a bag or your clothes.
  People who do this are called shoplifters.

pile
A pile of sweaters

## 10.3 EXPLANATIONS

### (a) Past Continuous
**Form**
was/were (+ . . . ing)

| Positive | Negative |
|---|---|
| I, he, she, it was walking | I, he, she, it wasn't walking |
| you, we, they were walking | you, we, they weren't walking |

| Interrogative |
|---|
| Was I, he she, it walking? |
| Were we, you they walking? |

It is often used to describe something that was already happening in the past and we choose the past continuous when the action we mention is incomplete.

*A:* What was the weather like yesterday morning?
*B:* It was fine. The sun was shining so I went for a walk.

*A*: Where were you when I called?
*B*: I was probably travelling home by tube.

The past continuous (was doing) is often used with the past simple tense to show that something happened in the middle of something else.
Brigitte saw a shoplifter while she was walking down Oxford street. Margaret rang the hotel while Brigitte was travelling home by tube.

**(b) Stop (+ infinitive) *vs* Stop (+ . . . ing)**

  (i) **Stop (+ infinitive)**
     To make a break and do something else.
     Brigitte stopped to look in a shop window. (She was walking and stopped to look.)
     I stopped to telephone home. (I was working and then I stopped to telephone.)

  (ii) **Stop (+ . . . ing)**
     To stop what someone is doing or does.
     Brigitte stopped looking at the shops. (She did something else.)
     I want to stop smoking. (It's bad for me. I want to stop.)

**(c) Adverbs**
An adjective tells us more about nouns.
Many adverbs are formed from adjectives by adding -ly to the end.

| Adjective | Adverb |
|-----------|--------|
| quick | quickly |
| slow | slowly |
| incredible | incredibly |

(note slight variation)

But remember that words like lonely, friendly, lively are adjectives.
Useful irregular examples are:

| Adjective | Adverb |
|-----------|--------|
| good | well |
| fast | fast |
| hard | hard |
| late | late |

We use adverbs to give more information about a verb. For example, we can say how something is done.

She walked slowly.

She did it well.

We also use adverbs before adjectives and other adverbs.

I was terribly tired. (adverb + adjective)

She did it incredibly quickly. (adverb + adverb)

## 10.4 BACKGROUND

### Shoplifting

In many of Britain's larger stores, customers are intended to serve themselves. The open shelves and attractive goods mean that people sometimes try to shoplift. This is a major problem. To stop this, many shops have security cameras, electronic stock control and store detectives.

In some shops there may be notices like this:

Shoplifters will be prosecuted.

And people who shoplift and are caught are usually taken to court. When the person is a foreign visitor with a lot of money, there is usually a lot of bad publicity. Theft in the high street is a major problem, which makes goods more expensive. Shop owners try their best to stop shoplifting but it seems more goods are taken by people who work in the shops than by shoplifters.

## 10.5 **EXERCISES**

### Section A

### Exercise 1
Complete the following sentences using verbs from the box. Use the past continuous form.

```
try   stand   leave   steal   walk
```

1 I . . . . . . down Oxford Street, late yesterday afternoon when something strange happened.
2 I saw a woman who . . . . . . things from a shop.
3 She . . . . . . the shop when she was caught.
4 Some people . . . . . . round the cash desk when I spoke to the manager.
5 As I walked in, I saw a woman who . . . . . . a sweater on.

### Exercise 2
Use the words in the brackets to make sentences using the past continuous.
(what/you/do/phone/rang?)
What were you doing when the phone rang?
1 (why/you/walk/Oxford Street/late yesterday afternoon?)
2 (she/not/really/try/clothes on)
3 (the security men/watch/the woman?)
4 (I/walk/quickly/I/be tired)
5 (you/window shop/at 4 p.m.?)

### Exercise 3
Put the verb into the past continuous or past simple.
Brigitte was walking (walk) down Oxford Street when she stopped (stop) to look at a shop window.
1 Brigitte . . . . . . (travel) home by tube when Margaret . . . . . . (telephone).
2 The woman . . . . . . (put) some perfume in her bag when Brigitte . . . . . . (see) her.
3 What . . . . . . (she/wear) at the time of the theft?
4 The woman . . . . . . (not/see) that Brigitte . . . . . . (look) at her.
5 I . . . . . . (stop) to look at a shop window.

6 While she . . . . . . . (put) some sweaters in her coat I . . . . . . .
  (go) to get the manager.
7 They . . . . . . . (arrest) her as she . . . . . . . (leave) the store.
8 I . . . . . . (watch) her from outside the shop for a few minutes.
9 Someone called Margaret . . . . . . . (telephone) ten minutes ago.

## Section B

### Exercise 4
There was a bomb at the station. Many people were there. Use the
words in brackets to answer the questions:
'What were you doing when the bomb exploded?'
'What did you do next?'
(I/wait/for/friend) (leave the station)I **was waiting for a friend and
when the bomb exploded I left the station.**
1 (I/sell/newspaper/stall) (call the police)
2 (I/collect/tickets) (run for help)
3 (I/wait/cousin) (go to look for her)
4 (I/buy/ticket) (got on my train)
5 (We/get off/train) (leave the station as quickly as possible)
6 (We/have a drink/restaurant) (we not leave our table)

### Exercise 5
Complete these sentences with an appropriate adverb which begins
with the letter(s) given.
1 I walked sl . . . . . . . down the street because I was tired.
2 The Sultan of Brunei is inc . . . . . . . rich.
3 He is a good worker because he always does things w . . . . . . .
4 Do you always drive so f . . . . . . . ? You are doing 160 kph.
5 He came in so qu . . . . . . . that I didn't hear him.
6 Martha has a lovely voice. She sings bea . . . . . . .
7 My hair was b . . . . . . . cut. I look terrible.
9 Please move this car . . . . . . . It might break.
10 Can I have another beer, please? This bottle is com . . . . . . .
   empty.

### Exercise 6
Make sentences to describe what you were doing at these times
yesterday.

| | | | |
|---|---|---|---|
| 06:30 | 11:00 | 16:30 | 20:30 |
| 08:30 | 13:00 | 17:30 | 11:00 |

**Writing**
You are Brigitte. You are writing to a friend. Use the dialogues in this Chapter to tell the story of your walk down Oxford Street. Use conjunctions like **while, next, after,** *etc.* to make the story clear. See page 220 of the reference section.

# WHAT'S HE LIKE?

## 11.1 DIALOGUES 📼

### (a) Dialogue 1

Margaret and Brigitte are still speaking on the telephone.

*Margaret*:   Anyway, my cousin Peter is expecting you and he'll be at the station to meet you.

*Brigitte*:   That's great! But how will I recognise him? What's he like?

*Margaret*:   Oh, Peter. Well, he's about 25, medium build and he's got wavy brown hair, and the last time I saw him he had a bushy moustache. He has been a researcher at the University for three years, so he looks very serious and academic. In fact, I'm pretty sure that he wears glasses now. You don't need to worry! He'll find you. Cambridge station isn't a very big place.

*Brigitte*:   I hope so, I don't want to go off with the wrong man!

*Margaret*:   That's a point! Look, I'll have to go. I'm meeting someone for dinner. I'll see you at the Balmoral on Saturday. Bye!

*Brigitte*:   Bye!

### (b) Dialogue 2

Later in the evening Brigitte meets Laurent in the lobby. He looks excited.

*Brigitte*:   Hello! What's up?

*Laurent*:   Linda Lovely's here in the hotel.

*Brigitte*:   Who?

*Laurent*:   Linda Lovely. You know, the actress and pop singer. She's been in quite a few of the tabloids recently.

*Brigitte*:   Oh! I don't read them. When I get an English paper I prefer 'The Times' or 'The Independent'. How long have you been here?

*Laurent*:   Since 9.

*Brigitte*:   So, what's so special about her?

*Laurent*:   Well, erm she's got long blonde hair and a beautiful figure and she's a really good singer. She's had several hits including 'Tonight I want to be with you!'.

*Brigitte*:   Is that her over there?

*Laurent*:   Where?

*Brigitte*:   The lady who has just come in.

*Laurent*:   Which one?

*Brigitte*:   The one with blonde hair.

*Laurent*:   Oh, come on, that's not her. The woman's almost forty!

*Brigitte*:   Does it matter? She's slim and attractive and very well dressed. Isn't she your type? Don't you like older women? I really can't understand how you men can get so excited about nothing.

*Laurent*:   Look, don't exaggerate. I just wanted to see what Linda Lovely looked like. After all, it isn't every day that we get a celebrity in the Balmoral. I expect she has already left.

*Brigitte*:   Who told you she was here?

*Laurent*:   A man in reception.

*Brigitte*:   Perhaps it was a joke.

*Laurent*:   You might be right. Look, why don't we have a quick drink in the bar?

*Brigitte*:   Why not!

## 11.2 VOCABULARY

### (a) Dialogue 1

**Useful expressions**

- To expect someone

   To wait for someone to arrive.

   I'll expect you at 8 p.m.

- That's great!

   Informal expression to express happiness.

- Medium build

   build = physique

   Your build is the size that your bones give to your body.

   You usually talk of small, medium and large build.

- I'm pretty sure
  pretty = very (in this example)
- To recognize someone (also spelled 'recognise')
  To know who someone is
  I recognized him from his photograph.

(ii) **Words to learn**
- researcher
  Someone who looks for new facts or information in a subject.
- academic
  An academic is a member of a university who teaches or does research. If you look **academic** it means you look like a university teacher.
- wavy hair
  Hair that is in waves. We also speak of straight or curly hair.

|     wavy     |   straight   |    curly     |

- a bushy moustache
  A bushy moustache is a thick one.

**(b) Dialogue 2**
  **(i) Useful expressions**
- What's up?
  What is going on?
- Don't exaggerate
  Don't make it more important than it is.
- I expect
  You can also use I **expect** when you think that something you say will be proved true.
  Who's that at the door? I expect it's Mrs Vine. She said she would come at 7 p.m.
- You might be right
  It is possible that you are correct.

  (ii) **Words to learn**
- actress
  Woman who appears in plays or films.

actor is the masculine.

- pop singer
  Person who sings modern music or pop.
- tabloids
  Popular newspapers (see 11.4)
- blonde
  Also spelt blond (especially when talking about men)
  Pale yellow coloured hair.
  We sometimes use a blonde to talk about a person with blonde hair.
  Marilyn Monroe was a blonde.
- hit
  A record (film, play, *etc.)* that is very popular
- attractive
  A person who is attractive is pretty (female) or handsome (male).
- celebrity
  Person who has become famous.

## 11.3 EXPLANATIONS

### (a) The present perfect tense

#### (i) Form

We form the present perfect with have/has (+ the past participle). Many past participles end with -ed. Others are irregular. There is a list on page 268.

| Positive | Negative |
|---|---|
| I/we/they/you have he/she/it has been | I/we/they/you haven't he/she/it hasn't been |

| Interrogative |
|---|
| Have I/you/we/they Has he/she it been? |

Note the contractions: **I've** = I have **She's** = she has.

(ii) **Uses**

We use the present perfect when there is a connection between the past and the present.

**Andrew has been a researcher at the University for three years.**

(He started three years ago. He is still there today.)

**I have had this flat since 1978.** (I moved here in 1978. I am still here.)

We also use it to talk about past events that have present importance. This may be 'news'.

**The President has been killed.**

or something that happened very recently

**She's just come in.**

just = a short time ago

**I've finished!**

We also use the present perfect + **already** when something happens sooner than we expect

**She's already left.**

**Have you already finished?**

We use the present perfect + **yet** in negative statements when we talk about something that has not happened up to the moment of speaking.

**He hasn't arrived yet.**

Sometimes (particularly with rising intonation) this expresses surprise; sometimes you are stating that it is going to happen. In questions **yet** is a way of finding out if something has happened up to the moment of speaking.

**Have you finished yet?**

**(b) Since vs For**

We use both **since** and **for** to talk about a period of time in which something has happened.

**Since** is used with a point in time.

**I've been here since 10 a.m.**

**For** is used with a period of time.

**I've been here for two hours.**

| Examples with since | Examples with for |
|---|---|
| 9 p.m.  Saturday  Easter 1968  he arrived | two weeks  an hour  one minute a long time  10 years |

## 11.4 BACKGROUND

### Newspapers

Britain is a major newspaper-reading country and the reader has a large number of national daily papers to choose from. The most popular papers are the tabloids. These are small-sized newspapers in which the articles are short, often with a lot of photographs. A lot of the news in the tabloids is not very serious and many of the headlines are sensational.

**MY STEAMY SHOCK IN SCHOOL SHOWER**

**Gym mistress claims male teacher peeped**

STAR REPORTER

SPORTS teacher Jane Matthews told yesterday how a male colleague burst in on her TWICE in the showers.

The first time Catholic school games master David Emsley allegedly ogled her she was still dressed in her undies.

But on the second occasion the gym mistress was starkers, an industrial tribunal heard.

"The second time it happened it was obvious I was in the shower. You could hear the water running," she said.

"He asked me what colour I wanted my walls painted. I glared at him and he left immediately."

**Misery**

Miss Matthews, 32, also told of pupils' sex and booze romps, affairs between staff, and a married woman teacher's illicit relationship with a boy at Harrytown High School, Romiley, Cheshire.

After reporting the saucy snooper to the headmaster, Miss Matthews, of Bredbury Green, Romiley, said her life at the school was made a misery.

She said there were embarrassing slanging matches in front of fellow staff and Mr Emsley swore at her on several occasions.

Miss Matthews, who claims constructive dismissal, added that a school governor even warned to be nice to Mr Emsley "or you won't get promoted."

She said: "I was being held to ransom."

The hearing continues.

MISS MATTHEWS: Glared

### Sensational headlines

Some of the better known tabloids are 'The Sun', 'The Daily Mirror' and 'The People'.

Newspapers like 'The Times', 'The Guardian', 'The Daily Telegraph' and 'The Independent' are known as the 'quality' papers. They cover a wide range of news and try to separate facts and opinion although all the national papers except 'The Independent' usually support one of the major parties. Other well-known papers are 'The Daily Express' and 'The Daily Mail'. These are neither as serious as the quality papers nor as sensational as the tabloids.

Some of these newspapers also publish Sunday editions with colour supplements.

There are also some important local newspapers which present local as well national news. However, many local papers are in financial trouble because of competition from free local newspapers which appear once a week.

Like so much else in Britain, the newspaper world is changing too.

## 11.5 EXERCISES

### Section A

### Exercise 1

Complete this dialogue with an appropriate form of the present perfect. The first example has been done.

*Laurent*: Hi! Have you seen (you see) Linda Lovely?
*Brigitte*: Who?
*Laurent*: Linda Lovely! She's a famous star and she's in the hotel.

*Brigitte*: How long . . . . . . . (she be) here?
*Laurent*: I'm not sure.
*Brigitte*: Well, I . . . . . . . (not seen) anyone who looks like a film
   star. . . . . . . . (you look) in the bar?
*Laurent*: Yes. She . . . . . . . (not be) in there.
*Laurent*: How about the dining room?
*Laurent*: I . . . . . . . (not look) there yet. I will.
*Brigitte*: Hey. Look at that woman who . . . . . . . (just come) in.
   Is she Linda Lovely?
*Laurent*: Of course she isn't. She hasn't got blonde hair.
*Brigitte*: I expect she . . . . . . (already leave). Let's go for a
   drink.

## Exercise 2
Make questions with the words given.
(you/spoke/to Brigitte/recently?) **Have you spoken to Brigitte recently.**
1 (she already/leave/the hotel?) ................................................
2 (you/just/come in?) ...........................................................
3 (you/eat/anything this evening?) ...........................................
4 (you/see/Linda Lovely in the last few minutes?) .......................
5 (they/finish/their meal yet?)..................................................
6 (you/have/your holiday for this year?) ...................................

## Exercise 3
Insert **already, yet** or **just** into the appropriate sentences.
1 Have you sent the book . . . . . . . ? I've already sent it.
2 Who is that woman who has . . . . . . . come in?
3 Have you . . . . . . . finished or did you finish earlier?
4 I haven't finished . . . . . . . I'll be another five minutes.
5 It's time to clean your room. I've . . . . . . . done it. I did it this
   morning.
6 Have you finished . . . . . . .? I didn't expect you to finish for
   another hour.
7 I don't know what the problem is. I've only . . . . . . . arrived.

## Section B

## Exercise 4

Which of these words describe any of the people in the photographs?

| | | | | |
|---|---|---|---|---|
| friendly | slim | attractive | old | young |
| serious | smart | old-fashioned | trendy | handsome |
| pretty | ugly | funny | cute | smart |

**Exercise 5**

Complete the following with a verb from the box. Use the simple past or the present perfect tense, as appropriate.

| work go build cross lose find do finish give |

1 In 1987, Richard Branson . . . . . . . the Atlantic in a balloon.
2 Nobody . . . . . . . the lost city of Atlantis yet.

3 He . . . . . . in the company for twenty years. He left in 1984.
4 People . . . . . . research on AIDS for several years now.
5 On Monday, I . . . . . . to Paris on business.
6 It's amazing! He . . . . . . a marathon in world record time and he isn't even tired.
7 He . . . . . . the house while he was living in Paris.
8 I don't believe it. I . . . . . . it to you yesterday and you . . . . . . it already!

**Exercise 6**
Insert **since** or **for** into the appropriate sentences.
**Where's John? Oh, he's been in America since 1987.**
1 Ladies and gentleman, he's been climbing . . . . . . six hours.
2 I haven't seen Peter . . . . . . Monday.
3 She hasn't been to work . . . . . . July.
4 He's been a student . . . . . . years.
5 I've been on holiday . . . . . . three weeks.
6 She has been playing with violin . . . . . . I arrived.
7 I've known him . . . . . . a long, long time.
8 He's been a friend of mine . . . . . . we were at school.

**Writing**
Look at the photograph of the old man on page 109.
Write a short description of him.
Include information about his face, his hair, his eyes and his clothes.
Compare your description with the one in the key.

# I'M SORRY I'M LATE...

## 12.1 DIALOGUES 📼

### (a) Dialogue 1

Brigitte is at Liverpool Street station. She has bought her ticket.

*Brigitte:*    Can you tell me where the train to Cambridge leaves from?

*Ticket clerk:*    It usually goes from platform 14. But it'll be up on the board. You'll have to hurry though. The train leaves in five minutes.

*Brigitte:*    What! My timetable says the train leaves at 8:40.

*Ticket clerk:*    Ah, that's the old time. The timetable has changed. But don't worry, if you hurry, you'll catch it.

Brigitte runs to platform 14.

*Brigitte:*    Is that the train to Cambridge?

*1st Ticket Collector:*    No, ma'am, 'fraid not. It's going from Platform 8 this morning. You'd better run.

Brigitte runs to platform 8.

*Brigitte*: Cambridge, please.

*2nd Ticket Collector*: I'm sorry, love. You've just missed it.

*Brigitte*: Oh no. There's someone waiting for me at the station.

*2nd Ticket Collector*: Well, don't worry. There's another train at 9:05.

*Brigitte*: What platform will it leave from?

*2nd Ticket Collector*: Let's have a look. Platform 14.

*Brigitte*: Are you sure? If I hadn't gone to platform 14 just now, I would have caught the train.

*2nd Ticket Collector*: It happens! Anyway it won't be long before the next one.


**(b) Dialogue 2**

Brigitte arrives in Cambridge. A man greets her.

*Peter*: Brigitte Scherer?

*Brigitte*: Yes, you must be Peter! How did you recognise me? Margaret said you had a moustache and glasses. You're quite different. I wouldn't have recognised you.

*Peter*: Margaret sent me a photograph last week. I got rid of the moustache last year and I'm wearing contact lenses now. Anyway, welcome to Cambridge. I've got my bicycle here but let's get a taxi to the centre. The station's a little way from the centre 'cos when the railway first came to Cambridge, the University authorities insisted that it should be kept outside the city limits.

*Brigitte*: Look, I'm terribly sorry I'm late. I didn't realize the timetable had been changed.

*Peter*: Don't worry. I haven't been here long. Did you have a good journey?

*Brigitte*: Not bad, I suppose. I would have caught the 8:40 if I hadn't gone to the wrong platform. I don't know what to say. I'm usually never late.

*Peter*: Look, don't worry. How were you supposed to know that they had changed the timetable? I've gone to the wrong platform before, too! They sometimes change things at the last moment and that can be a bit embarrassing if you haven't left much time.

*Brigitte*: Yes, I'd have got to the station a little earlier if I had known about the changes in the timetable.

*Peter*: Well, never mind. You're here and that's all that matters. Look, here's a taxi now. Let's go and see a bit of Cambridge.

## 12.2 **VOCABULARY**

### (a) **Dialogue 1**

#### (i) **Useful expressions**

- You'll have to hurry

  If you have to do something, you must do it.

  So, you'll have to is a way of telling someone what they must do.

  You'll have to rush. (= hurry)

  You'll have to leave.

- Ma'am

  Short form for madam. A way of addressing a woman you don't know.

  Madam (for women) and sir (for men) are relatively formal.

- I'm afraid not

  Expressions like I'm afraid not or I'm afraid or I'm afraid to say are ways of apologizing (as in this example) or disagreeing politely.

  A: Can you come to lunch next Sunday? B: I'm afraid I'm busy.

  A: Well, what do you think? B: I'm afraid I don't agree.

- You'd better

  You'd better (+ infinitive) is a polite way of telling or advising someone

  You'd better be careful.

- Love

  Very informal way of addressing a woman.

  = dear. Not to be used.

- To miss (a train, boat, *etc.*)

  To arrive too late.

#### (ii) **Words to learn**

- Platform

  The area in a station where you get on or get off a train.

- Board

  Here it means the indicator board which lists the time of arrivals and departures in stations (or airports).

  We often use board for a word that includes board in its name.

  Black board, notice board, *etc.*

- to catch

  To arrive in time for a plane or train, *etc.*

  I have to leave to catch my train.

  It's very late. Do you think he'll catch his plane?

## (b) Dialogue 2
### (i) Useful expressions
- I got rid of
  When you get rid of something you don't want, you remove it, sell it, give it away or throw it away.
  A: I got rid of my old car last week.
  B: What did you do with it?
  A: I sold it for £20.
- I'm terribly sorry
  Terribly is an adverb. Used to emphasise that Brigitte is sorry. Useful form of apology.
- I didn't realize
  If you realize something, you become aware of it.
  After a few minutes, I realized that the woman in blue was Margaret Thatcher.
  So, I didn't realize means I didn't know or I had no idea.
- Did you have a good journey or not?
  Used to greet someone who has arrived after travelling from one place to another. (a journey or trip)
- I suppose
  Here Brigitte uses I suppose because she is not sure whether it was a good journey or not.
- How were you supposed to know?
  If something is supposed to happen it is planned to happen.
  We use supposed to especially when things go wrong.
  Dinner was supposed to be at 8, but we didn't eat till 10.
- It can be embarrassing
  = something to make you feel shame or guilt.
  It was very embarrassing for me to lose all my clothes.
- Never mind
  Here = it is not important.

## 12.3 EXPLANATIONS

### (a) If I hadn't done X, I would (n't) have done Y (3rd conditional)
Brigitte missed her train because she went to the wrong platform. If she hadn't gone to the wrong platform, she wouldn't have missed the train.

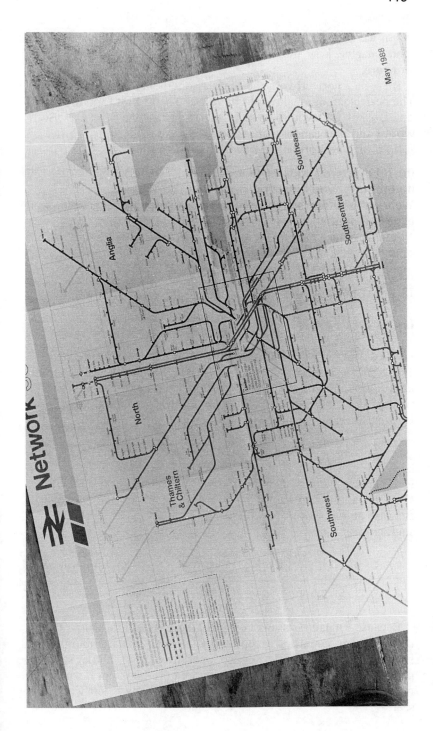

When we want to talk about things that did not happen in the past (and imagine how things might have been different) we use the structure:

If (+ past perfect) with the perfect conditional (see page 265).
The perfect conditional **would have done** is the past form of **would do**. Do not use **would have** in the **if** part of the sentence. Both **would** and **had** can be contracted to **'d**.

**If I'd arrived earlier, I'd have caught the train.**

**(b) If (+ present) with the future**
**If you hurry, you'll catch it.**
We use this form when there is a real possibility that something will happen in future.
Note that we use the present in the **if** part of the sentence, not a form of **will**.

## 12.4 BACKGROUND

**Intercity transport**

Liverpool Street is one of the large main-line stations in London. Trains from Liverpool Street serve the Eastern Region. Other important London stations are Waterloo, Charing Cross and Victoria (which serve the South); Paddington (which serves the West) and Euston, St. Pancras and King's Cross which serve the Midlands and the North). Rail travel is an important form of Intercity travel. Intercity trains which run between the main cities are usually fast and frequent and the trains are modern. However, because Britain has had an extensive railway network since Victorian times, some of the smaller stations and suburban trains are very old and run down. Because of this, British Rail is spending a lot of money improving its stations and trains.

Coach travel is cheaper than rail travel and for certain journeys it can be faster. The main coach terminal in London is at Victoria, and passengers can book coach travel to most cities and towns.

Because England is a small country, there is less internal air travel than in many countries except between cities like Edinburgh and London where a shuttle service operates. In a shuttle service, passengers can arrive at the airport without pre-booking. If a plane is full, the airline provides another plane, so nobody is left without a seat.

# WELCOME TO THE BEST OF BRITAIN!

THERE'S NO BETTER, FRIENDLIER WAY TO SEE BRITAIN AND THIS YEAR WE'VE INCLUDED ALL YOUR OLD FAVOURITES WITH LOTS OF NEW TOURS TOO.

NO MATTER WHAT YOUR PREFERENCE OR POCKET – THERE'S SOMETHING TO SUIT EVERYONE ON A NATIONAL HOLIDAY.

## VALUE FOR MONEY

When you choose **National Holidays** you choose real value for money. Just look what you get, and it's all included in the holiday price.

- LUXURY COACH TRAVEL
- FREE LOCAL DEPARTURES
- ALL HOTEL ACCOMMODATION

## – SEE WHAT WE INCLUDE!

- FREE EXCURSIONS
- INDIVIDUALLY RESERVED SEATS
- EXPERIENCED DRIVER/COURIERS
- **NATIONAL HOLIDAYS** REPUTATION AND RELIABILITY

## NATIONAL HOLIDAYS

## DEPOSITS

| HOLIDAY | Deposit | Insurance Premium |
|---|---|---|
| British (SPRING) | £15 | £5 |
| British (SUMMER) | £20 | £6 |
| Jersey & Ireland | £30 | £12 |

(Holiday Insurance premiums are additional to tour cost.)
THE ABOVE DEPOSIT AND INSURANCE PREMIUM (IF REQUIRED) ARE PAYABLE AT THE TIME OF BOOKING.

## REGIONAL CENTRES

| MIRY LANE, WIGAN LANCASHIRE WN3 4AG | GEORGE HOUSE GEORGE STREET WAKEFIELD WF1 1LY |
|---|---|
| ☎ ADMINISTRATION (0942) 44246 | ☎ ADMINISTRATION (0924) 383838 |
| ☎ RESERVATIONS (0942) 824824 | ☎ RESERVATIONS (0924) 387387 |

VIEWDATA: (0942) 824224 OR ISTEL NETWORK 1312 #

## 12.5 EXERCISES

**Section A**

**Exercise 1**
Put the verb in the correct form.
If Brigitte **had known** (know) about the new timetable she would have arrived earlier.
**She would not have gone** (not/gone) to platform 14 if she had looked at the board.
1 If Brigitte . . . . . . (look) at the board she might have caught the train.
2 She . . . . . . (not/hurry) if the ticket clerk hadn't told her about the new timetable.
3 She . . . . . . (not/recognize) Peter without a moustache if he hadn't spoken to her.
4 She . . . . . . (arrive) earlier if she had caught the train.
5 Peter wouldn't have recognized Brigitte so easily, if Margaret . . . . . . (not/send) him a photograph.

**Exercise 2**
Write an appropriate sentence with if after each statement.
Brigitte missed the train because it left from platform 8.
**If the train hadn't left from platform 8, Brigitte wouldn't have missed it.**
1 Brigitte arrived late in Cambridge because she missed the train.
   If ...............................................................................
2 Brigitte missed the train because they changed the platform.
   If ...............................................................................
3 Peter was able to recognize her, because Margaret sent him a photograph.
   If ...............................................................................
4 Peter and Brigitte took a taxi because it was too far to walk.
   If ...............................................................................
5 The University insisted that Cambridge station be built outside the city walls.
   Cambridge station ...............................................................

**Exercise 3**
Write an appropriate apology or excuse for each situation.
You are late. You missed the train because of a new time.
**I'm sorry. The timetable had changed.**

1 The train left from platform 8. It wasn't your fault.
  I'm sorry ...............................................................
2 You forgot to bring the photographs. You were in a hurry.
  I'm afraid ..............................................................
3 Someone is speaking Spanish to you. You can't understand.
  I'm sorry ...............................................................
4 You were speaking German to someone. She wasn't German and
  didn't speak German.
  I'm so sorry, I didn't realize ...............................................
5 You have just broken a priceless cup. You don't know what to say.
  I'm terribly sorry...........................................................

## Section B

### Exercise 4
Match the two parts to make one sentence.
1 If the weather is warm . . . . . . .     A if you hadn't gone.
2 If the weather were warm . . . . . . B people will come.
3 Margaret will go . . . . . . .          C if you went with her.
4 If the weather had been warm . . . D if you go with her.
5 Margaret wouldn't have gone . . . .E people would come.
6 Margaret would go . . . . . . .        F people would have come.

### Exercise 5
You are planning a European trip. Tell a friend what you will see in
each place.
Paris/Eiffel Tower
**If I go to Paris, I'll see the Eiffel Tower.**
1 Pisa/Leaning Tower.
2 Venice/St Mark's Square.
3 Madrid/Prado.
4 Amsterdam/canals.
5 Athens/Acropolis

### Exercise 6
Laurent's last holiday was a disaster!
The food was bad, the weather was bad, the hotel was being built,
there was no water in the pool, he was lonely, *etc.*
But the holiday was cheap, it was winter, it was a new resort, he went
alone *etc.*
Make sentences similar to this one.
**The food would have been better if he had paid more.**

## Writing

On your return from holiday on 15th June you find the following letter about some books you ordered

---

**R Cooper**
**Booksellers**
**6 The Crescent**
**Bidicombe**
**Devon**

**Telephone: 0770 2139   Fax 21345   Telex: 3194 COOP R**

10th May 19..

R James
2 Field Road
London SW1 2DJ

Dear Mr James,

We wrote to you on 3rd March asking you to pay a deposit on the enclosed order for books. We have not heard from you and unless we receive payment by 1st June we shall have to cancel the order.

Yours sincerely,

R Cooper

---

Write a letter of apology to Mr Cooper.
1  Acknowledge his latest letter.
   Thank you for your letter of . . .
2  Explain you did not receive the letter of 3rd March.
   I am afraid . . .
3  Apologise for the delay.
   I am sorry . . .
4  Give your excuse.
5  Provide the solution.
   I enclose . . .
6  Sign off with an appropriate ending.
   A version of this letter is on page 222.

# THAT'S KING'S COLLEGE

# ON THE LEFT

## 13.1 DIALOGUES

### (a) Dialogue 1
Brigitte and Peter arrive at King's College.

*Taxi driver*:  Right, I'll just pull up in the space ahead. That's
  King's College on the left.
*Peter*:   Here you are. Keep the change.
*Taxi driver*:   Thanks. Have a good day, sir.

*Brigitte*: He must think that you're a tourist.

*Peter*: We do get a few. Well, as the man said, the gate in front is the main gate of King's College. If you go through to the courtyard I'll tell you a little bit about it.

*Brigitte*: Gosh, it's lovely.

*Peter*: Yes, it is rather nice. Have you heard of the Carol Service from King's College chapel?

*Brigitte*: No, I haven't.

*Peter*: Well, every Christmas Eve there's a Carol Service from the chapel and millions of people watch it on television or listen to it on the radio. The building on the right is the chapel and it is one of the most beautiful buildings in the world.

*Brigitte*: How old is it?

*Peter*: Well, King's was founded by Henry VI as a religious and academic foundation around 1441, but the Chapel wasn't completed until the 1540s during the reign of Henry VIII. That was when he added the towers, but it's the inside which is really rather special. There's some sixteenth century stained glass by English and Flemish glaziers, as well as a magnificent fan vault ceiling. Come on. Let's go and have a look.

### (b) Dialogue 2

Peter and Brigitte come out of King's College.

*Peter*: Well, what did you think?

*Brigitte*: From the inside, it really is one of the most beautiful chapels I've ever seen. How did they get the Rubens over the altar?

*Peter*: Well, it was purchased at an auction in 1961 and given to the College. The buyer wanted the masterpiece to find a permanent home in Britain. I'm not sure I like it.

*Brigitte*: It is a very powerful painting. Have you seen many of his paintings?

*Peter:* A few. Anyway, we'll go and have a look later at the famous view of King's from the Backs, which are the gardens between the colleges and the river Cam. I'd like to show you around my College next.

*Brigitte*: Fine, where to?

*Peter*: Well, I'm at Clare and that in fact is the College on the left. Clare was founded in 1326 but most of the buildings date from the seventeenth century. We can get to it through this gate here.

*Brigitte*: Lead the way.

## 13.2 VOCABULARY

### (a) Dialogue 1

#### (i) Useful expressions

- **to pull up**
  To make a vehicle slow down and stop.
- **Have a good day, sir**
  An expression which is widely used in American English.
- **It's lovely**
  It's very attractive.
- **It was founded**
  If someone founds something, they start it up.
  **Henry VI founded Eton and King's College Chapel.**
- **come on**
  Invitation to follow.

#### (ii) Words to learn

- **gate**
  A door-like structure (at the entrance to a garden, a collection of buildings, *etc.*)
- **courtyard**
  Flat open area surrounded by buildings. Many Cambridge Colleges have courtyards.
- **Carol Service**
  Carol = religious song that people sing at Christmas
  Service = religious ceremony
- **tower**
  Tall, narrow building. Many churches and castles have towers.
- **century**
  Period of 100 years
- **glaziers**
  Glass makers
- **fan vault ceiling**
  Ceiling found in many buildings from the Middle Ages.

**(b) Dialogue 2**

(i) **Useful expressions**

- lead the way

  Show me where to go and I'll follow.

- to date from

  Made in or starting from a particular time.

  The building dates from 1901.

- to purchase

  To buy something. More formal than to buy.

(ii) **Words to learn**

- masterpiece

  A very fine work of art (painting, book, film, statue, *etc.*)

  One day, I'm going to paint my masterpiece.

## 13.3 EXPLANATIONS

**(a) The passive**

Henry VI founded King's College in the fifteenth century. (active)

King's College was founded in the fifteenth century. (passive)

(i) **Form**

In passive sentences we use the correct form of the verb to be (is, are, was, have been, will be, might have been, *etc.*) (+ the past participle).

The passive -ing form is being (+ past participle).

The room is being cleaned.

We often use the passive when:

- The person (or thing) that did something is not so important.

  The towers of King's College Chapel were built at the time of Henry VIII.

- The person (or thing) that did something is not known.

  My money was stolen this afternoon.

**(b) The sixteenth century**

A century is a period of a hundred years.

The sixteenth century refers to the years starting 1500.

The twentieth century refers to the years starting 1900.

**(c) Have you ever heard of . . .?**

We can use the present perfect to connect the past with the present.

For example, in this exchange

*A*: Have you ever been to Cambridge?

*B*: No, I haven't.

*A* is talking about *B's* life up to the present moment.

In this use of the present perfect we often use **ever** or **never**.

I've never had a car.

I've never smoked.


## 13.4 BACKGROUND

**University life**

Cambridge is a market town as well as a centre for computer industry but it is best known as a university town. It is one of the oldest and most famous British universities. The other is Oxford. They were founded in the 13th century.

Oxbridge is the colloquial term for Oxford and Cambridge. The education in Oxbridge is said by some to be superior to that in the other universities but others may not agree! Until very recently, students from Oxbridge held many of the key jobs in public life. Although Oxbridge is very well known, there are in fact 46 universities in Britain.

- There are Oxford and Cambridge;
- There are universities founded in the nineteenth century like London and Manchester;
- There are the newer universities like Essex and Lancaster. These are often known as red brick universities

Polytechnics are colleges where students get further or higher education. The demand for higher education means that many of the 30 or so polytechnics give degrees too. The courses in polytechnics usually have a greater emphasis on technical and vocational subjects such as business management and engineering.

Oxbridge is a series of independent colleges. For example, in Cambridge there are 25 colleges. Together they form the university, which is governed by the Senate.

King's College is just one of the Colleges.

Some of the other universities also have independent colleges. In others there are departments.

The Oxbridge colleges are famous for their architecture. Many have chapels and lovely dining halls. Many of the colleges also have a courtyard and very beautiful gardens although some of these are only for the Fellows (a Fellow is senior member of a college; usually a professor).

Undergraduates are students studying for their first degree. First degree courses leading to a B.A. or B.Sc., usually take three years.

In Britain, the majority of undergraduates get a grant. The amount depends on the income of the parents. If parents do not earn much money, the students get a full grant.

Students often live in a college for part of their student years and most of the Oxbridge colleges are residential. Lectures take place in modern buildings known as faculties. However, in Oxbridge (and a few other universities), teaching is based on tutorials, and lectures may be optional. A tutor (a university teacher) sees the students either individually or in small groups, and gives them work to do on their own. This work is then handed in and discussed with the tutor.

## 13.5 EXERCISES

### Section A

### Exercise 1

You are asking about someone's life and interests up to the present.
Use the words in brackets to make your questions.
(you ever/see/any of Ruben's paintings?) Have you ever seen
any of Rubens' paintings?
1 (you/ever/be/to China?) ...................................................
2 (you/read/any of Shakespeare's plays) ...............................
3 (who's the most interesting person/you/ever/meet?) ..................
4 (you/never/do/anything wrong?) ........................................
5 (you/ever/try/steak and kidney pie?) ...................................
6 (you/ever/hear/of/King's College Chapel? ............................

### Exercise 2

Make a passive sentence with the words in brackets.
King's College Chapel is a lovely old building. (when/it/build?)
When was it built?
Be sure to choose the right tense.
1 The picture in the Chapel is a Rubens masterpiece. (purchase/in
1961)
...........................................................................................
2 Is the College very old? (yes/to be founded/in/sixteenth century)
...........................................................................................
3 Did Henry VI see the final building? (no/finish/about 100 years
after his death)
...........................................................................................
4 We can't go into that building. (it/paint/at the moment)
...........................................................................................
5 When will they finish? (the building/finish/sometime next year)
...........................................................................................

### Exercise 3

Make a passive sentence which keeps the same meaning.
Henry VIII completed King's College Chapel.
King's College Chapel was completed by Henry VIII.
1 Somebody stole my money yesterday afternoon.
My money ...........................................................................
2 They are painting the College.
The College ........................................................................

3 They changed from platform 14 to platform 8 at the last moment.
  The platform ................................................................
4 They have changed the room for the meeting.
  The meeting room ..........................................................
5 Somebody met Brigitte at the station.
  Brigitte .......................................................................
6 The air crash killed twenty people.
  Twenty people ..............................................................
7 Will they discover a cure for AIDS soon?
  Will a cure ..................................................................

## Section B

### Exercise 4

Match these inventions with the dates and make sentences about
when they were invented.

**The telephone was invented in 1876.**

| | | | |
|---|---|---|---|
| a | Gunpowder | 1 | 1945 |
| b | Atomic bomb | 2 | 1608 |
| c | Screw | 3 | 1903 |
| d | Paper | 4 | 200 B.C. |
| e | Printing | 5 | 1885 |
| f | Telephone | 6 | 1000 |
| g | Microscope | 7 | 1876 |
| h | Motor car | 8 | 1440 |
| i | Aeroplane | 9 | 105 |

Choose 5 of the inventions and make sentences about the century
they were invented in.

**The telephone was invented in the nineteenth century.**

### Exercise 5

Use the correct form of **compose, discover, invent, paint,** or **write**
in the passive and match the columns. The first one has been done.

**The Ninth Symphony was composed by Beethoven.**

| | | | |
|---|---|---|---|
| a | The Ninth Symphony | 1 | Tchaikovsky |
| b | Dynamite | 2 | Louis Pasteur |
| c | The telephone | 3 | Charles Dickens |
| d | Hamlet | 4 | Alexander Bell |
| e | The smallpox vaccination | 5 | Leonardo da Vinci |
| f | The gramophone | 6 | The Chinese |
| g | Gunpowder | 7 | Thomas Edison |
| h | The Nutcracker Suite | 8 | Shakespeare |
| i | The Mona Lisa | 9 | Beethoven |
| j | Bleak House | 10 | Alfred Nobel |

**Exercise 6**
Write these questions with a superlative adjective and then answer them.
(which/be/large/city/in your country?)
Which is the largest city in your country?
1 (who/be/popular/actor/in your country?)
................................................................................................
2 (when/be/the/good/time/to visit your country?)
................................................................................................
3 (which/beautiful place/ever/visit?)
................................................................................................
4 (what/be/interesting/book/ever/read?)
................................................................................................


**Writing**
Choose a famous building and write a brief description answering these questions.
Who built it?
When was it built?
Why was it built?
What is special about the building?

# CHAPTER 14

# WHAT'S UP? ARE YOU FEELING WELL?

## 14.1 DIALOGUES 📼

### (a) Dialogue 1

Brigitte has arranged to meet Hank in the hotel.

*Hank*: Hello, Brigitte. How was your trip to Cambridge?

*Brigitte*: It was wonderful. Have you ever been?

*Hank*: No, I haven't.

*Brigitte*: Well, you must. But, what's up? Are you feeling OK? You don't look very fit.

*Hank*: I'm not. I hardly had any sleep last night.

*Brigitte*: Oh, dear! What was the matter?

*Hank*: Well, I didn't feel very well when I went to bed but I got to sleep, and then at about 1 a.m., I woke up with a terrible headache and a pain in my side. I just couldn't get back to sleep.

*Brigitte*: How do you feel now?

*Hank*: A bit better, the pain's still there but it isn't as bad as it was.

*Brigitte*: Well, if I were you, I'd go and see a doctor.

*Hank*: Gee, no. I'll be OK.

*Brigitte*: Why not? It can't do any harm. There is a special doctor for hotel residents and you're insured, aren't you?

*Hank*: Yes, of course I am.

*Brigitte*: Then it's settled. Why don't you ring the doctor for an appointment now?

**(b) Dialogue 2**

Hank telephones the doctor's surgery.

*Receptionist*: Dr Moore's surgery. Good morning.

*Hank*: Er, good morning. I'd like to make an appointment to see a doctor, please.

*Receptionist*: Have you been to this surgery before?

*Hank*: No, I haven't. In fact, I'm a visitor to this country.

*Receptionist*: That's OK. Could I have the name, please?

*Hank*: Yes, it's Byam, Hank Byam.

*Receptionist*: Can you spell that for me please?

*Hank*: Byam. B-Y-A-M.

*Receptionist*: And the address?

*Hank*: The Balmoral Hotel.

*Receptionist*: When would you like to come?

*Hank*: Well, I felt awful last night.

*Receptionist*: You'd better come today. Can you make it at 2:30 this afternoon?

*Hank*: Yes, I can.

*Receptionist*: Do you know where to find us?

*Hank*: Yes, there's a map in the hotel.

*Receptionist*: OK. See you at half past two. Bye.

*Hank*: Goodbye.

**(c) Dialogue 3**

Hank is at the doctor's.

*Doctor*: Come in, Mr Byam. Sit down. I believe this is your first visit?

*Hank*: Yes, I'm on holiday.

*Doctor*: We'll go through your history later. Now what appears to be the problem?

*Hank*: Well, I developed a terrible pain in my stomach at about one o'clock last night.

*Doctor*: What sort of pain was it? Was it sharp? Dull?

*Hank*: It was very sharp.

*Doctor*: How long did this last?

*Hank*: About twenty minutes.

*Doctor*: Have you still got a pain?

*Hank*: It's a lot better.

*Doctor*: Right, let me have a look at you.

## 14.2 VOCABULARY

### (a) Dialogue 1
#### (i) Useful expressions
- How was your . . .?
  A common greeting when you see someone after they have
  been somewhere. (a trip, a weekend, or even an interview)
  How was your weekend?
- I hardly . . .
  I hardly slept means I almost did not sleep at all.
  A: Did you like your dinner?
  B: No, I hardly ate anything at all.
- What was the matter?
  What's the matter? or Is anything the matter? are used to
  find out the reason for a problem. You use it when someone
  looks different from usual. For example when they look sad,
  tired, or worried.
- How do you feel?
  = How are you now?
- If I were you, I'd go
  Way of giving someone advice.
  A: Where do you think I should go on holiday?
  B: If I were you, I'd go to Ireland.
- Why not?
  A way of asking the reason.
- It can't do any harm
  A way of recommending action which you think will be good.
  It can't do any harm to be nice to your boss
  Well, this new job won't do you any harm.
- You are insured, aren't you?
  The tag aren't you is used to check information. See page 199.
- That's settled
  That's decided. When someone settles an argument or problem
  they end it by taking a decision.
  After two weeks, the strike was settled by a pay increase.
- Why don't you go?
  Why (+ not) can be used to introduce a suggestion.
  Why don't you eat a few of these cakes?

#### (ii) Words to learn
- fit
  If you are fit, you are healthy and able to take exercise without
  feeling tired.
  Most footballers are very fit.

- pain
  A bad feeling in your body from illness or injury.
  Where is the pain?
  She had pains in the stomach.
- headache
  A pain in your head.
  A: I have a bad headache.
  B: Take an aspirin.
- appointment
  An arrangement to see someone at a special time. Usually to do with work.
  Can I see Mr Jones, please? I have an appointment at 1 p.m.

## (b) Dialogue 2
### (i) Useful expressions
- I'd like to make an appointment
  When you make an appointment, you ask to see someone at a particular time and day.
  We also say to make a reservation
- You'd better (do something)
  = You should (do something)
- Can you make it at 2:30 p.m.?
  Can you arrive by the appointed time, which is 2:30 p.m.?
- See you.
  See you and See you later are informal ways of saying goodbye when you expect to see someone again in a short time.

### (ii) Words to learn
- surgery
  Place where a doctor or dentist sees patients.
  I waited for a long time in the doctor's surgery.
- awful
  Not very good or nice.

## (c) Dialogue 3
### (i) Useful expressions
- What appears to be the problem?
  General question which aims to get the patient to describe the problem.
- How long did it last?
  To last = go on for, in time
  A football match lasts 90 minutes.

(ii) **Words to learn**
- history
  In this context a history is a record of the patient's health.
  The doctor had trouble taking the patient's history. The patient couldn't remember anything.
- terrible
  very bad
- dull
  Pain which is dull is not very definite. You find it hard to say exactly where the pain is coming from.
  She had a dull pain in her stomach for several days before she went to a doctor.
- sharp
  A sharp pain is deep; it hurts and it is easy to locate.
  Roger felt a sharp pain in his arm. He looked and saw a deep cut.

## 14.3 EXPLANATIONS

### (a) Advice
Often, when we give advice we try to get people to do things for their own good. There are many ways of doing this in English. Here are some of them.
If I were you I should . . .
Quite often we give advice by making a conditional sentence with the expression if I were you.
If I were you, I should go to the doctor.
I shouldn't do that, if I were you.
We usually use should rather than would although the contraction 'd is common in conversation.
Sometimes we don't use If I were you . . .
I should see a doctor.
I shouldn't do that.
In this case the I should means: I think you should
The form we choose depends on the nature of the advice and the person we are talking to.

(i) **Strong forms for giving advice**
   You'd better . . . (+ infinitive)
   You should . . . (+ infinitive)
   If I were you I should . . . (+ infinitive)
   Have you tried . . . (+infinitive or +–ing)
   Why not . . . (+ infinitive)
   You could . . . (+ infinitive)

Have you ever thought of . . .(+–ing)
I was wondering if you'd ever thought of . . .(+–ing)

(ii) **Less certain forms**
Many of these forms are usually followed by the infinitive or
(–ing) form.
You'd better stop smoking.
Have you tried giving up cigarettes?

## 14.4 BACKGROUND

### Health

Hank, like many travellers, has private medical insurance. Most UK
residents depend on free treatment by the National Health Service

Who reinvests all profit today, to give you better health care tomorrow?

Who's developing special nursing homes to care for the elderly?

Who's working with the NHS and has provided it with a £1 million lithotripter to remove kidney stones without surgery?

Who's meeting the needs of the elderly, the sick, convalescents and new mothers as well as hospitals and industry with 24 hour professional nursing services?

Who's pioneering preventive medicine through the largest network of health screening centres and opening more every year?

Who's running modern, sophisticated hospitals, setting new standards in patient care and building even more?

Who's taking health screening out to the community with a fleet of mobile units and providing occupational health services to companies?

Quite simply, BUPA.

You see, BUPA has no shareholders to pay. So after taking care of our members' needs today, we can re-invest any surplus to help care for their needs in the future.

Well over three million people benefit from the peace of mind of BUPA membership.

Individuals looking after their families, the self-employed safe-guarding their livelihoods and com-panies large and small wanting the best for their employees.

It's hardly surprising that most people choosing private health care join BUPA.

If you would like to know how you can benefit from BUPA health care, please call 01-200 0200.

**BUPA**

Britain feels better for it.

Provident House, Essex Street, London WC2R 3AX.

(NHS) although the number of private medical insurance schemes is growing. Some NHS services are free to visitors, and travellers from the European Community have special rights, but visitors should check their own position before they travel.

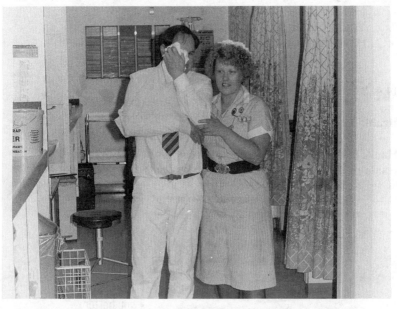

Emergency treatment is available from the Casualty Departments or larger hospitals. Many people get to the Casualty Department by car, taxi, or on foot, but more serious cases come by ambulance.

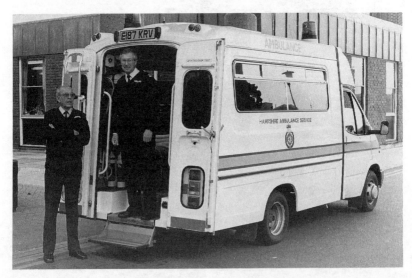

You can get an ambulance by telephoning 999 and asking for the ambulance service. (You use the same number to call the Police or Fire Brigade).

In Britain, the first doctor you see is usually a general practitioner (GP). A GP is a family doctor who is a specialist in general health. Usually, you make an appointment to see a GP at a surgery or health centre and if you have a special problem the GP will send you to a specialist.

If a doctor decides you need medicine, you will get a prescription to take to chemist's. In Britain, many medicines are available on prescription only.

If you have trouble with your teeth you can ask to see a dentist. Many dentists are very busy and it can be difficult to get an appointment. You can find a list of dentists and denture repairers (dentures are false teeth) in the 'yellow pages.' ('The yellow pages' is a telephone directory which lists companies under the services they offer.) Lists of doctors can also be found in the yellow pages.

For new glasses or contact lenses you should go to an optician. There is usually at least one optician on most British High Streets.

## 14.5 **EXERCISES**

### Section A

**Exercise 1**
A friend of yours looks very ill. What advice would you give him/her? Complete the sentences below.
1 If I were you I'd ...........................................................
2 You'd better ...............................................................
3 You should ................................................................
4 Why don't you .............................................................

Your boss is having trouble with a very old car which he/she likes. What advice would you give him/her?
1 Have you thought of .......................................................
2 It might be an idea to .....................................................
3 Do you think it's time that you ...........................................

**Exercise 2**
Match the words in column A with those in column B.

| A | B |
|---|---|
| 1 I've lost my credit card. | A Why don't you send her some flowers? |
| 2 I don't think I'll have time to get to the doctor. | B Have you tried counting to 1000? |
| 3 I can't sleep. | C Have you ever thought of moving? |
| 4 My wife is very angry with me. | D You'd better report the loss. |
| 5 It takes me hours to get to the office. | E If I were you, I'd go. |

**Section B**

**Exercise 3**
Where were the requests in column A made? Match them to the places in column B.
The first example has been done for you.

| A | B |
|---|---|
| 1 I'd like an appointment to see a doctor, please. | A A doctor's surgery. |
| 2 I'd like to arrange for my eyes to be tested. | B A restaurant. |
| 3 I'd like to book two seats for this evening's performance. | C A bank. |
| 4 Could I have an appointment with Mr Jones? My front tooth has broken. | D An optician. |
| 5 I'd like to see the manager about a loan. | E An airline office. |
| 6 I'm ringing to reconfirm my reservation on flight 210. | F A hotel. |
| 7 Can I make a reservation for the nights of April 21 and 22? | G A dentist. |
| 8 I'd like a table for two. | H A theatre. |

**Exercise 4**
Use **had better** or **had better not** in these situations.
A friend is at a party. He has to drive home. He wants another drink.
**You'd better not have another drink.**

1 It has started to rain. Your friend is about to go out without an umbrella.

......................................................................................

2 A friend is taking a train. It leaves in 10 minutes. You think she should hurry.

......................................................................................

3 Your friend is going to a foreign capital. You know that it is dangerous to go out in the streets at night.

......................................................................................

4 Someone you know is arriving at the airport. The taxis are very expensive but there is a very good bus service.

......................................................................................

**Exercise 5**

Use **should** or **shouldn't** to give advice to a friend who:
1 eats too much and is overweight.
2 spends a lot of time watching television.
3 never takes any exercise.
4 has a very old car that always breaks down.
5 is very unhappy in his/her job.
6 had some very exciting experiences during a journey around the world.
7 writes and sings some lovely songs in her spare time.

**Writing**

This is part of a note from a friend who works in your field in Britain. Write a reply to your friend's question.

> . . .As you know I would be interested in coming to work in your country next year. Do you think it would be possible? Whom should I contact? Any advice would be very welcome . . .

# I'M AFRAID I'VE GOT A COMPLAINT

## 15.1 DIALOGUES 📼

### (a) Dialogue 1

Brigitte sees Hank at breakfast.

*Brigitte*:   How are you this morning?

*Hank*:   A lot better. The pain's disappeared and I had a good night's sleep.

*Brigitte*:   What did the doctor say?

*Hank*: Well, she examined me and couldn't find anything wrong. It must have been something I ate.

*Brigitte*:   Well, I'm glad you're feeling better.

*Hank*:   So am I.

*Brigitte*:   Tell me, did you have any hot water in your room this morning?

*Hank*:   I sure did, why?

*Brigitte*:   Well, the water hasn't been very hot since I arrived but this morning it just ran cold.

*Hank*:   Well, I would go and complain.

*Brigitte*:   I think I'll do it now.

### (b) Dialogue 2

Brigitte goes to reception. There is a new receptionist.

*Receptionist*:   Can I help you?

*Brigitte*:   Yes, I'm afraid I've got a complaint. There wasn't any hot water in my room this morning.

*Receptionist*:   Oh, dear. What is your room number?

*Brigitte*:   205 on the second floor.

*Receptionist*:   Just hang on for a minute. I'll give maintenance a ring.

Hello, maintenance. This is reception. I have a lady from room

205 with me. She didn't have any hot water in her room this morning . . .

Well, when will it be repaired?

Right, thank you.

I'm terribly sorry. The pump has broken down and they have to get a new one.

*Brigitte*: So, when will it arrive?

*Receptionist*: Unfortunately, it won't be till tomorrow. It's coming from Birmingham.

*Brigitte*: Look, I'm sorry, but I must have hot water. How am I going to wash my hair without it?

*Receptionist*: I can understand your problem, but there's nothing I can do.

*Brigitte*: How can you say there's nothing you can do? That's just not good enough. I mean, there's hot water in the other parts of the hotel. Could you move me?

*Receptionist*: I'm afraid the hotel's full, but I can give you a key to one of the bathrooms in the old building.

*Brigitte*: That's not very satisfactory.

*Receptionist*: I realise that, but it's the best we can do in the circumstances and it would only be for a day or two.

*Brigitte*: I think we ought to get compensation.

*Receptionist*: That's something you'll have to discuss with the manager. He'll be in in half an hour. I'll get him to look out for you. Meanwhile, would you like a bathroom key?

*Brigitte*: I suppose it's better than nothing.

*Receptionist*: Fine, I'll show you where it is, myself.


**(c) Dialogue 3**

Later that day. Brigitte is in a café. She has just received her bill.

*Brigitte*: Excuse me, I think there's been a mistake. I only had one coffee, not two.

*Waiter*: Oh, I'm terribly sorry. I'll go and do it again.

It seems we gave you the bill for table 14! It happens when it's busy.

*Brigitte*: That's all right, it doesn't matter.

*Waiter*: Did you enjoy your sandwich?

*Brigitte*: Yes, it was excellent, thank you. No complaints. Here, keep the change.

*Waiter*: Thank you. Enjoy the rest of your stay.

*Brigitte*: Thank you.

## 15.2 VOCABULARY

### (a) Dialogue 1

#### (i) Useful expressions

- **To have a good night's sleep**
  This means to sleep well without any disturbance.
  *It's very quiet here. I hope I have a good night's sleep.*
- **It must have been**
  A way of saying that we are quite sure about the reason something happened in the past. (see page 264)
- **I'm glad**
  = happy and pleased
- **So am I**
  Way of agreeing with a previous statement.
  *A:   I'm hungry.*
  *B:   So am I. I haven't had breakfast.*
- **Tell me**
  A useful way of introducing a new subject or topic of conversation.
- **The water ran cold**
  Water runs out of a tap. When we say the water is running cold we mean that hot water is not coming from the hot tap.

#### (ii) Words to learn

- **to examine**
  To look at something/someone closely.
- **complain**
  If you complain, you tell someone about a problem, in the hope they will do something about it.

### (b) Dialogue 2

#### (i) Useful expressions

- **I'm afraid (I've got a complaint)**
  I'm afraid there's . . . is one of the most common ways of expressing a complaint and I've got a complaint is understood.
  *I'm afraid there is no soap in my room.*
- **Hang on**
  Informal way of asking someone to wait for a moment.
- **I'm terribly sorry**
  A very common way of beginning an apology.
  *I'm terribly sorry but I've lost your passport.*

- **Unfortunately**
  You often use this adverb to introduce bad news.
  Unfortunately, the theatre is full. I can't get tickets.
  Can you come tonight? No, unfortunately, I can't.
- **I can understand your problem (but) . . .**
  Way of saying that you want to help but you can't.
- **How can you . . .?**
  How can and how could are ways of showing that what you have heard is very silly or stupid.
  How could you say anything so silly to your boss?
  How can you say you are poor? You have a huge house and good job.
- **That's just not good enough**
- **That's not very satisfactory**
  These are ways of asking for a better solution to your complaint.
- **I realise**
  I understand your reason.
- **In the circumstances**
  Use this expression to show that what you are saying is the result of your thinking about a situation or problem.
  In the circumstances, I think you should leave.
- **It's the best we can do**
  Way of presenting a final offer
- **I suppose, it's better than nothing**
  Very weak form of agreement. Brigitte doesn't like the solution but decides there is nothing she can do except move to another hotel.

(ii) **Words to learn**
- **maintenance**
  = keeping a building or machine in good condition so that it works well.
- **pump**
  = a device to move a liquid (water, gas, *etc.*) from one place to another.
- **repair**
  To mend something that is not working.
- **compensation**
  Payment from an organisation (here the hotel) for something bad that happens.
  The flight was 12 hours late but all the passengers got compensation from the airline.

**(c) Dialogue 3**

  (i) **Useful expressions**

- Excuse me, I think there's been a mistake . . .
  Polite way of introducing a complaint.
- It seems . . .
  It appears.
- It happens when it's busy
  Something which happens is something which occurs without a plan. So,
  It happens or It can happen can be used as an apology or explanation.
  Well, I don't know how the car crashed. It just happened.
  *A*: I'm sorry, I've broken your vase.
  *B*: Don't worry, it can happen to anyone.
  That's all right, it doesn't matter
  Way of accepting an apology. (See page 147)

  (ii) **Words to learn**

- excellent
  very very good
- sandwich
  Two or more slices of bread with food in between

## 15.3 EXPLANATIONS

**(a) Must**

  (i) **Form**

    Must is a modal verb.
    It does not have an infinitive or participles.
    We use must to talk about the present and future.
    It does not have a past tense.

| Positive | Interrogative | Negative |
|----------|---------------|----------|
| I must<br>He/she must<br>You must *etc.* | Must I . . .?<br>Must he . . .?<br>*etc.* | I must not<br>He/she<br>   must not *etc.*<br>   (also mustn't) |

    Must is followed by the infinitive (without to.)
    I must leave

(ii) **Uses**

1 Must is used to give strong advice or orders (sometimes to oneself).

I must have hot water.

I must stop smoking.

2 You must (do) something means it is necessary for you to do something.

It's late. You must leave.

You mustn't (do) something means you should not do something.

Sh! You mustn't talk. He'll hear us.

3 We can use have to instead of must, in all forms including the past.

Did you have to go?

Sometimes, when we use have to we are reporting a fact.

I have to work on Friday.

When we use must the speaker is telling what he thinks is necessary.

I must go and see my mother. I haven't seen her for a month.

*Note:* mustn't and don't have to have different meanings.

You mustn't means you should not do something.

Don't have to means it is not necessary.

4 Must can also be used when we are sure about something (because it is logically necessary)

What is 2 + 2? It must be four.

Who's that? It must be Paul. It's seven o'clock.

We use the perfect infinitive for deductions about the past.

It must have been the food I ate.

It must have been Paul. It's his bag.

*Note:* In this sense we only use must in the positive.

For the negative and question forms we use can.

It can't be true.

Can it really be anyone else?

**(b) Complaints**

A direct verbal complaint often sounds very rude, so we normally introduce a complaint less directly with expressions like:

I'm afraid there's a small problem, the . . .

Look, I'm sorry to bother you, but . . .

I'm sorry to have to mention this . . .

Excuse me, I'm afraid there's been a small mistake . . .

### (c) Apologies

The basic form of apology in English is to say **Sorry**. Sometimes however, you may need to go further with expressions like:

I'm awfully sorry.

I'm terribly sorry. It won't happen again.

I can't tell you how sorry I am.

I'm so sorry. I just don't know what to say.

I'm ever so sorry. I do apologise.

These are some ways of accepting an apology.

Don't worry.

Don't worry about it.

It doesn't matter.

That's all right.

Never mind.

Let's forget it.

It happens.

### 15.4 BACKGROUND

**How to put things right**

In England most businesses are very helpful when you complain and they will try and do something when you complain that goods are faulty (*i.e.* have something wrong with them).

The three shopping rules are:

1 Goods must be of merchantable quality. A new item must not be broken or damaged. It must work properly.

2 It must be as described on the package, the display sign or by the seller. For example, shirt sleeves should not be long if marked 'short' on the box.

3 Goods must be fit for the stated purpose. If the shop says something will work, it should.

But what should you do if you want to complain?

1 Stop using faulty goods.
2 Tell the shop at once.
3 Take it back yourself (if you can).
4 Take a receipt or proof of purchase (if you can).
5 Ask for the manager or owner.
6 Keep calm!

The shop should offer you a replacement or a refund (your money back). You don't have to choose another item.

If you have no luck and need help, go the local Citizen's Advice Bureau or Tourist Information Centre for advice.

## 15.5 EXERCISES

### Section A

### Exercise 1

Complete these sentences with **must** or **have to** (in its correct form). Sometimes you can use **must** or **have to**. Sometimes only one of them is possible.

I'm sorry. I **must/have to** have hot water to wash my hair.
I didn't feel very well last night. I **had to** get up several times.

1 I'm afraid I . . . . . . . go. I'm late for my train.
2 Why did you . . . . . . . get up last night? Were you not well?
3 I . . . . . . . stay in my room because the hotel was full.
4 The pump needed a new part. It . . . . . . . come from Birmingham.
5 He . . . . . . . stay at reception all day tomorrow.
6 Next year, I . . . . . . . go to America on business although I'm not keen on the idea.
7 I . . . . . . . try to stop smoking. It's bad for me.

### Exercise 2

Read the situation and write a sentence with **must have**. Use the words in brackets.

Hank was unwell. The doctor could not find anything wrong with him. (It must/be/something he/ eat)
**It must have been something he ate.**

1 Why is there no hot water? (the pump/must have/break down again)
. . . . . . . . . . . . . . . . . . . . . . . . . . . . . . . . . . . . . . . . . . . . . . . . . . . . . . . . . . . . . . . . . . . . . . . . . . . . . . .

2 Laurent wasn't at breakfast. His table was empty. (he/must have/ already/finish)

...............................................................................................

3 I had one coffee not two! (Oh dear/I must have/give you the wrong bill)

...............................................................................................

4 Did you see Linda Lovely last night? (no/she/must have/leave/ before I/arrive)

...............................................................................................

5 Did you hear the noise last night? (no/I must have/be/asleep)
No,.........................................................................................

6 Laurent's late for class again! (he/must have/lose/his way)

...............................................................................................

**Exercise 3**
Read the situation and write an appropriate complaint or apology.
Use the expressions to help you.
You are late for a meeting. You missed the train.
**I'm sorry I missed my train.**
1 You are in a hotel. The hot water has stopped running.
I'm afraid ................................................................................
2 You receive the bill in a restaurant. There is a mistake.
Excuse me, I ...........................................................................
3 You are in a friend's house. You have broken a vase. You think it might be very expensive.
I'm terribly ............................................................................
Is it .................................................................................... ?
4 You are in a crowded hotel reception. You sit down in a chair. Then, you realize that it is somebody's seat.
................................. I didn't realize .............................
5 You had a meeting. You forgot. The person telephones. Suggest a meeting for next week.
I'm ever ...............................................................................
6 You go to your garage to collect your car. It still doesn't work. You go back again. Tell them and find out what they are going to do.
Look, I'm sorry but .................................................................

**Section B**

**Exercise 4**
Write down what you might say in these situations.
You are in a restaurant. Your soup is very cold. Complain to the waiter.
**I'm afraid this soup is rather cold. Could you heat it up, please?**

150

1 Your friend is a few minutes late for a meeting. She is usually on time. She lost her way. She apologizes. What do you say?

..................................................................................................

2 Your boss lends you a book. He wants it back. You realize you left it on a plane. You will buy another copy.

..................................................................................................

3 It is the end of a play. People are collecting their coats. You notice, a very important person has taken your coat.

..................................................................................................

4 You bought a new radio two days ago. You can't get it to work. You take it back to the shop.

..................................................................................................

5 You are late for an important meeting. You left home very early but there was a bad accident on the motorway.

..................................................................................................

6 You have spilt some wine on the carpet during somebody's party You want to clean it up.

..................................................................................................

7 You are in a queue for theatre tickets. Someone tries to get in the queue in front of you.

..................................................................................................

8 Someone pours coffee on you. It's a very old suit ready for cleaning. They apologize. What is your reply?

..................................................................................................

9 A person in your office is always late. You want him/her to improve. This morning he/she is late again. What is your reply to 'I'm sorry I'm late!'

..................................................................................................

10 You are in a restaurant. You have been waiting for some time. The waiter is chatting. You want to be served.

..................................................................................................

**Exercise 5**
Use **must/can/can't have** to complete these sentences.
I asked at the hotel but she isn't registered any more.
**She must have left.**
1 He'll return the book as soon as he finds it, but he hasn't.
He ..................................................................................................
2 He should have stopped at the traffic lights but he didn't.
He ..................................................................................................
3 I'm looking for my cheque book. I don't know where I put it.
Where ..............................................................................................?

4 You have a meeting with a colleague. It isn't in his diary.
He ................................................................................
5 You get back to your car. The radio is gone.
Someone ................................................................................
6 Your friend looks very angry. It was something a friend said.
What ................................................................................
7 A man starts a job that takes 10 hours. After two hours he says
'I've finished!'
You ................................................................................

**Exercise 6**
In each situation below you receive an apology. Accept the apology
and say something to make the person feel better.
Someone has poured soup on your white tablecloth. This is not the
first time and the table cloth washes well.
**Don't worry, it will wash. It's happened before.**
1 Someone has lost a book of yours. You have several copies.
2 Your secretary has forgotten to bring a document to a meeting.
You won't need it.
3 Someone apologises for not remembering your name. This is a
problem for you too.
4 Someone apologises because they only have coffee and no tea. You
can't drink coffee.
5 A dinner guest breaks one of your plates.

**Writing**
You bought a stereo radio/cassette recorder last Saturday. When you
got home you found the radio did not work.
Write a letter of complaint. Include the following:

(i) **Background**
  * what did you buy?
  * when did you buy it?
  * where did you buy it? (shop, branch + a copy of any
    receipts)

(ii) **The problem**
  * what has gone wrong with it?

(iii) **The solution you want**
  * repair? replacement? your money?
  Finish off politely. For example, I look forward to hearing
  from you.

# CHAPTER 16

# IN THE OLD DAYS WE USED TO . . .

## 16.1 DIALOGUES 📼

### (a) Dialogue 1

Brigitte and Margaret go to spend the weekend with Margaret's grandmother in Yorkshire. She is showing them round the house.

*Grandmother*: And this is your room. I hope you don't mind sharing. I don't have a lot of space. But when you're alone you don't need it.

*Brigitte*: I'm sure we'll be fine.

*Grandmother*: The bathroom is just over there.

*Margaret*: Have you had it redone?

*Grandmother*: No, not yet. It's still very old-fashioned and it needs doing but I haven't got round to it. When you get older, things take a lot of time . . . but, you know, when I was a young girl we didn't have an inside toilet or bathroom. We used to go outside, and once a week I used to have a hot bath in the kitchen, near the stove! Anyway, you don't want to listen to an old woman, do you?

*Brigitte*: Yes, I'd be really interested.

*Grandmother*: That's very sweet . . . I won't go on but I've got some photographs of Margaret I can show you later!

*Margaret*: Thanks!

*Grandmother*: Let's finish our tour first. If you go through the kitchen you can have a look at the garden. It's past its best. I used to do a lot but I can do less and less these days. I have a man who comes to help me about twice a week. Come on. Let's go out for a while.

*Brigitte*: It's wonderful. There's so much colour.

**(b) Dialogue 2**

Grandmother is showing Brigitte and Margaret some old photographs.

*Grandmother*: This is one of Margaret when she was 7.

*Brigitte*: What were you doing?

*Margaret*: Well, when I was a child, I used to go down to my uncle's farm for all my holidays, and I think I must have been waiting to milk one of the cows . . .

*Grandmother*: Here's another one. She's a little older now.

*Margaret*: Do you like the uniform?

*Brigitte*: It suits you . . .

*Margaret*: I was very proud of it. I used to be very keen, you know. I think I've still got the uniform somewhere. I shouldn't think it fits any more, though.

*Brigitte*: I didn't know you were a Girl Guide.

*Margaret*: That was ages ago. I'd left before I went to University. I'd grown out of it.

*Grandmother*: Yes, things change. Ah yes, this is one of the old house . . . You see we used to live in a large Victorian semi in Leeds. That's where Margaret's mother and her sisters grew up, but when the girls left home and my husband retired, we looked for a cottage in the country and came here. We had only been here for about four years when Albert died, but I decided to stay. Mind you, it's beginning to be a bit difficult. I'm not as young as I used to be.

## 16.2 VOCABULARY

**(a) Dialogue 1**
  **(i) Useful expressions**
  ● To show someone round (a house)
    When someone shows you round, they point out all the useful or interesting parts on a first visit.
    I went to the new flat yesterday. I was shown round by a young man.

- **I hope you don't mind**
  If you do not mind, you are not annoyed or bothered.
  *A:* I'm sorry I've lost your hat.
  *B:* Don't worry. I don't mind. I never liked it.
- **I'm sure we'll be all right**
  One way of indicating you don't mind.
  *A:* I'm afraid the room is very small.
  *B:* Oh, I'm sure we'll be all right.
- **To have something redone**
  To do something again to improve it.
  *A:* This is the wrong colour.
  *B:* Well, we'll have it redone.
  **It needs doing**
  If something needs doing it means some form of action or repair will improve it.
- **To go on**
  To continue talking.
  He went on and on. I couldn't stop him.
- **It's past its best**
  Here, the garden is no longer at its most beautiful.

(ii) **Words to learn**
- **To share a room**
  To use a room with another person
  I shared a room with my sister until we were six.
- **old-fashioned**
  The bathroom is old-fashioned because there are now bathrooms which are much more modern and up-to-date.
- **inside toilet**
  A toilet inside a house rather than in a separate room outside.
- **stove**
  Something for cooking or heating a room.

(b) **Dialogue 2**
  (i) **Words to learn**
- **to milk**
  To get milk from a cow, goat *etc.*
- **a guide**
  A Guide or Girl Guide is a member of the Girl Guide Association. This is an Association of girls similar to the Scouts, which is a worldwide organisation for boys. Guides aged 7–10 are called Brownies from the colour of their uniform. Boys from 8–10 are Cubs.

- to grow out of something
  To become too big or mature to do or wear something any more.
  **I grew out of sucking my thumb when I was five. He still does it.**
- keen
  If you are keen, you are very enthusiastic about something and spend a lot of time on it.
  **I'm a keen tennis player. I always play twice a week, sometimes more.**
- to fit
  To be the right size.
  **Does the new shirt fit?**
- Victorian
  Things made or built in England in the 19th Century, when Victoria was the Queen of England
- semi
  A **semi** is a semi-detached house. This is a house joined to the one next door by a shared wall. (see page 158)

## 16.3 EXPLANATIONS

**(a) Used to**
We use **used to** (+ the infinitive) when something was a habit in the past but no longer happens today.
**I used to play football every Saturday but I gave up three years ago.**
**I used to smoke a lot but now I only smoke after a special meal.**
We also use **used to** for a situation that does not exist today.
**We used to live in Leeds.**
**Covent Garden used to be a vegetable market. Today it's an area of fashionable shops and restaurants.**
The structure only exists in the past.
Although we can say. Used you to smoke . . .? the form Did you use to smoke? is more usual as is the negative form
**I didn't use to live . . .**
I used not to live . . . is also possible.
Note the way **used to** is pronounced on the tape.

**(b) Past perfect (I had left)**
  **(i) Form**
      Had (+ past participle)

(ii) **Meaning**

When we are talking about the past.

I went to university.

We use the past perfect to talk about something that had already happened before.

I had left the Guides before I went to university.

She had left before I arrived.

It is also the past of the present perfect.

| Present perfect | Past perfect |
|---|---|
| We have been here for three years. | We had been here for three years (when he died). |

## 16.4 BACKGROUND

**Housing**

In Great Britain, families prefer to live in houses rather than in flats (apartments).

Over 70% of people live in a whole house and only about 20% live in flats.

About 35% of people own the house they live in, or are buying it with money borrowed from a bank or building society. This is known as having a mortgage.

## Types of housing
### (i) The terraced house

Terraced houses are attached to each other in a long row. They are usually found in towns and cities and many were built in the 19th or early 20th century as housing for workmen. Today, Victorian terraced houses are very popular city homes. In earlier times, terraced houses were also called town houses. These have three or four storeys and very large rooms, and town houses are now very expensive and fashionable.

### (ii) The semi-detached house

In the 1930's a large number of semis were built. They share a central wall. Typically, a semi has a small garden in front and a fence divides a larger garden at the back. Semis are still built where land is expensive. This is a plan of a semi on a modern housing estate.

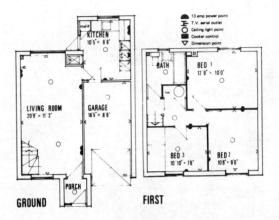

## (iii) The detached house

A detached house has land all round it. More and more modern homes are detached, although in areas where building land is expensive, the houses may be very close to each other.

## (iv) The country cottage

Country cottages are often old stone buildings which were part of a farm. Some country cottages are very old and they may have a thatched roof. Today many people who work in the cities buy cottages so that they have a place to go for the weekend.

## (v) A bungalow

A bungalow is a house where all the rooms are on the ground floor. As there are no stairs, many older people dream of going to live in a bungalow when they retire.

(vi) **A block of flats**

In the 1950s and 1960s many tower blocks of flats were built. Except for a few luxury developments, flats have not been popular in England. People do not like to live in them and there have been many social problems. Many blocks of flats are derelict and empty, and very few new ones are built today.

(vii) **The country mansion**

Very few of the British live in country mansions. Today many mansions are used as restaurants, hotels, old people's homes, *etc*.

Many British people are lucky enough to live in their own house, and the great majority of these have a small garden. However, housing is a problem in many cities. Many young people have to live in, or share, small one-room flats called bedsitters, and the homeless are still a problem.

## 16.5 EXERCISES

**Section A**

**Exercise 1**
Complete these sentences with used to (+ infinitive).
Margaret used to be a Girl Guide.
1 Margaret . . . . . . . to a farm for her holidays.
2 Margaret . . . . . . . a cow during her farm holiday.
3 Margaret's grandmother . . . . . . . a big house in Leeds.
4 She . . . . . . . the garden alone but she needs help now.
5 She . . . . . . . with her husband but she's alone now.

**Exercise 2**
Complete these sentences about Margaret's grandmother.
1 Margaret's grandmother used to live in a big house but today
. . . . . . . . . . . . . . . . . . . . . . . . . . . . . . . . . . . . . . . . . . . . . . . . . . . . . . . . . . . . . . . . . . . . .
2 Grandmother used to live in a town but today . . . . . . . . . . . . . . . . . . . . . . .
. . . . . . . . . . . . . . . . . . . . . . . . . . . . . . . . . . . . . . . . . . . . . . . . . . . . . . . . . . . . . . . . . . . . .
3 She used to do the garden but today a man . . . . . . . . . . . . . . . . . . . . . . . . . .
. . . . . . . . . . . . . . . . . . . . . . . . . . . . . . . . . . . . . . . . . . . . . . . . . . . . . . . . . . . . . . . . . . . . .

**Exercise 3**
Complete these sentences using the verb in brackets.
By the time Margaret went to University she (leave) had left the
Guides.
1 She wasn't there when I arrived, she . . . . . . . (go) already.
2 I . . . . . . . (finish) my work when it was time to go.
3 When they met me they . . . . . . . (not see) me in 20 years.
4 By the age of 11 he . . . . . . . (write) his first symphony.
5 I explained that I . . . . . . . (forget) my passport.
6 I didn't recognize him although I . . . . . . . (meet) him once
before.
7 I understood the moment I saw him that he . . . . . . . (have) an
accident.

**Section B**

**Exercise 4**
Match Part A to Part B. The first example has been done for you.

| A | B |
|---|---|
| 1 Covent Garden used to be a vegetable market . . . | A today it's a fashionable area of shops and restaurants. |
| 2 Ronald Reagan used to be an actor. . . | B before he went to live in America. |
| 3 The Republic of Zimbabwe . . . | C before settlers arrived in 1788. |
| 4 Ivan Lendl used to live in Czechoslovakia . . . | D in the nineteenth century. |
| 5 The museum at the Quai D'Orsay in Paris . . . | E used to be known as Rhodesia. |
| 6 Australia used to belong to the aborigines . . . | F but in 1980 he became the US President. |
| 7 Children used to work in coal mines . . . | G used to be a railway station. |

Now write 6 similar sentences about people and places in your country.

**Exercise 5**
One day when you got home you found this!

It was a surprise party. What had your friends done?
They had baked a cake.
Write sentences explaining what else they had done.

**Exercise 6**
Find some old postcards, photographs or prints of the town you live in. Use the structure **used to** to make sentences about the major changes.
There used to be a market but it's now a car park.

**Writing**
A recent article in a magazine said this about the lifestyle of British children in the 1930's.

*Transport*
Adults and teenagers used to use bicycles but they were too expensive to give to 10-year-olds.
They used to walk to school and came home for lunch. Private cars were rare and many couldn't afford public transport.

*Music*
There was no music specifically for children. Children used to listen to their parents' choice on the wireless.

*Clothes*
Children had three sets of clothes. They used to wear the best for church, second best for school and old clothes for playing.

*Bedtime*
They got up between 6:30 and 7:30. With no television, a cold house and poor light, bedtime was early; from 7 to 7:30 p.m.

What was life like for you as a child?
Did you get money as a child? What time did you go to bed? Did you have transport? Did you have your own music?
Write about what you used to do as a child.

# HOW TO MAKE YORKSHIRE PUDDING

## 17.1 DIALOGUES 📼

### (a) Dialogue 1

Brigitte, Margaret and Margaret's grandmother are in the kitchen.

*Margaret*: What's for lunch today?

*Grandmother*: Well, I thought as Brigitte's visiting, we'd have beef. I got a lovely piece of meat from the butcher and I'm going to roast it.

*Brigitte*: English roast beef is world famous.

*Grandmother*: You're right, my dear, but have you ever had Yorkshire pudding?

*Brigitte*: No, but I've heard of it. You eat it with roast beef, don't you?

*Grandmother*: That's right, but in the old days it was served first as a way of filling you up before you got to your main meal of meat and vegetables. If you come back later I'll show you how to make it. I'll just put the beef into the oven.

*Brigitte*: Can we help?

*Grandmother*: There's nothing left to do now. You can give me a hand with the vegetables later.

### (b) Dialogue 2

About an hour before the meal, Grandmother calls Brigitte and Margaret.

*Grandmother*: Girls, I'm ready to put the pudding in . . .

*Margaret*: Coming.

Margaret and Brigitte go in the kitchen.

*Brigitte*: What have you done so far?

*Grandmother*: Well, I've made the mixture. Basically this is a batter, which is a mixture of flour and milk. I put about four ounces of flour and a small teaspoon of salt into a bowl. Make sure there are no lumps in the flour. I then added an egg, a tablespoon of melted butter and half a pint of milk and I beat the mixture until it's quite thick. I then add the rest of the milk and let it rest. Now as you can see, I've pre-heated the oven to 220 degrees centigrade. Now, be a darling and pour some of the fat into this baking tin here.

*Brigitte*: Do you mean this fat here?

*Grandmother*: Yes, it's from the beef. You can use butter but I'm used to using the dripping. Now, put the pan in the oven. As soon as the tin smokes gently, we'll pour the batter in. In the meantime we'll have a look at the beef.

*Margaret*: Hmm, it looks fantastic.

*Brigitte*: Do you think it's hot enough?

*Grandmother*: Just a little longer, the secret of Yorkshire pudding is a hot oven. Otherwise the pudding won't rise.

*Brigitte*: How about it now?

*Grandmother:* That's great. Put it in the middle of the oven. Let's get the vegetables done. Do you like carrots?

Half an hour later.

*Grandmother*: Let's see how it's doing. It looks fine. We'll just lower the temperature slightly and wait for it to go golden brown. It should be ready in about 15 minutes.

## 17.2 VOCABULARY

### (a) Dialogue 1
#### (i) Useful expressions
- A (lovely) piece of meat
  A piece = a portion of something to eat
  Give me a piece of bread, please!
  I'd like that piece of chicken, please.
- World famous
  Known everywhere in the world
  Buckingham Palace is world famous.
- Fill you up
  To satisfy a hunger.
- To give someone a hand
  To help someone

(ii) **Words to learn**
- to serve (food and drink)
  To give people something to eat or drink.
  She served soup as a first course.
- butcher
  Person who prepares and sells meat.
- oven
  Part of a cooker
- to roast
  To cook something in dry heat in an oven or over a fire.
  We roasted a chicken for dinner.
  This is roast duck.

## (b) Dialogue 2

### (i) Useful expressions

- To beat something till it (thickens, rises *etc.*)
  To beat = to mix thoroughly with a fork or whisk.
  To thicken a liquid = to make it more solid.
- To leave something to rest
  To go away from, and not touch something for a period of time.
  In the meantime
  The period from now until something happens (here it means
  until the pan of fat is hot enough)
  I'm going to America next week; in the meantime I'll finish
  my book.
- The secret is . . .
  The best way to do this is . . .
- Get (the vegetables) done
  To cause something to be done. Here, the vegetables need to
  be prepared.

### (ii) **Words to learn**
- mixture
  Two or more substances mixed together
- ounce
  Unit of weight used in UK and US. 1 ounce (oz) = to 28.35
  grams
- teaspoon
  A small spoon that you use to put sugar into coffee and tea. So
  a teaspoon(ful) is the amount you can put in a teaspoon.
- bowl
  A round dish for food
- lump
  A piece of a solid substance

- tablespoon
  A large spoon used for serving food on a plate
- melted
  to melt = change by heat from solid to liquid
  The ice melted in the sun.
  Butter is usually solid. Melted butter is liquid.
- pint
  A measure for liquid = 568 cc
  (In America 1 pint = 473 cc)
- to pre-heat an oven
  To make the oven hot before putting the food in
- to bake
  To cook in the oven without extra liquid or fat
  A baking tin is a tin in which you bake cakes, *etc.*
- dripping
  Fat that comes from meat when it is being cooked. Some
  people use this fat again.
- to smoke
  The fat is so hot it begins to burn
- otherwise
  You use otherwise to emphasize the result or consequence of
  doing (or not doing something).
  You'll have to get to work earlier, otherwise you might lose
  your job.
- to rise
  To increase in size and volume so it becomes higher.
  Cakes rise when they are cooked.
- to lower
  To decrease or make less
- slightly
  Just a little

## 17.3 EXPLANATIONS

**(a) be used to (I'm used to . . .)**
be used to can be followed by a noun or an (–ing) form.
I have lived in a city all my life, so I'm used to the noise.
My wife doesn't cook, so I'm used to cooking for myself.
It can be used in the past, present or future form.
It is quite different in meaning from used to do.
I used to play cards at work = I played cards at work before but I
don't any more.

**I'm used to playing cards at work** = I do this so often that I now do not find this strange any more. It has become a habit.

**(b) Imperatives**
1 **Add** some milk to the bowl.
2 **Be** quiet!
3 **Don't drop** the glass!
4 **Try** to sleep.
5 **Have** a drink.
These verbs are examples of imperatives.
The form of an imperative is the infinitive without **to**.
We use the same form to talk to two or more people.
Its uses include (1) instructions (2) orders (3) warnings (4) encouragement and (5) informal offers or invitations.
The negative form is **Do not** or **Don't**.
We can use **do** if we want emphasis in polite requests, complaints or apologies.
**Do tell me!**
**Do be quiet.**
Sometimes we also use **you** before the imperative. This is quite common when we give spoken instructions.
**You add milk, then you put the bowl in** . . .
Although the imperative doesn't have a subject we can use a noun or a pronoun in order to make it clear whom we are talking to.
**Brigitte, put the tin in the oven, please.**
**Somebody, help!**
The adverbs **always** and **never** come before the imperative.
**Always pre-heat the oven** . . .

## 17.4 BACKGROUND

### The regions of England

The British Isles is the name given to England, Scotland, Wales and Northern and Southern Ireland. It is a geographical term.
The United Kingdom or the UK is shown on the map. It consists of England, Scotland, Wales and Northern Ireland.
Although the UK is relatively small, the regions are quite different.

### (a) The South East
This is the most densely populated and prosperous area of Britain. London is the capital and the centre of business but most people who work in London commute there by train.

The new M25 motorway and easy communication to Europe means that the South East is likely to continue developing in future. Although the population is dense there is a lot of countryside. For example, the county of Kent is known as the garden of England. Well-known towns in the South East include Canterbury, with its famous Cathedral, the coastal resorts of Brighton and Eastbourne, the Channel ports of Dover, Folkestone and Southampton, which is one of the UK's busiest ports.

## (b) The North/North East/North West
The North has had many economic problems in recent years. Large towns like Liverpool, Manchester, Leeds, Sheffield, Newcastle, *etc.* used to be very important centres for manufacturing industries like textiles, engineering and shipbuilding. Today these industries are

much less important and people need to learn new jobs. Unemployment is higher in the North than the South. The cost of houses is lower. Some politicians talk of the North/South divide.

Although industry was and is very important, the North has some very beautiful scenery. The Lake District is a beautiful area of lakes and mountains. In contrast the Yorkshire Dales are wild and bare.

York and Chester were important Roman towns which now attract many visitors. Durham is an ancient university town with a small Cathedral.

## (c) The Midlands

The heart of England. Birmingham, the second largest city in the UK, and Coventry, its near neighbour, are the most important towns. The Midlands have been the centre of the engineering industries since the nineteenth Century. Despite this, agriculture has always been quite important in Shropshire, Worcestershire and Leicestershire.

Visitors to the Midlands go to Stratford-on-Avon, the birthplace of Shakespeare, Oxford, the famous university town, and Coventry to see the modern Cathedral.

## (d) East Anglia

East Anglia is very flat. A lot of the region is very quiet and rural. Cambridge, well-known as a university city, is also an agricultural centre and the centre of the computer industry. Norwich is the most important town in East Anglia.

## (e) The South West

The South West is mainly agricultural, although Bristol, Portsmouth and Southampton are industrial. Many people go to spend their holidays in Somerset, Devon and Cornwall. Bath, which is in Avon, is a very attractive town.

## 17.5 EXERCISES

### Section A

### Exercise 1
Use the information in Dialogue 2 to complete these notes on how to
make Yorkshire Pudding.

#### How to make Yorkshire Pudding

**You need**
1 . . . . . . . of flour.
2 . . . . . . . milk.
3 A . . . . . . . of salt.
4 . . . . . . . . . . . . . . .

**Method**
5 Make sure the flour . . . . . . . . . . . . . . . ..
6 . . . . . . . the flour, . . . . . . and . . . . . . in a bowl.
7 . . . . . . . the mixture until . . . . . . ..
8 . . . . . . . the rest of the milk.
9 . . . . . . . the oven to . . . . . . . . .
10 . . . . . . butter or . . . . . . . into a baking tin.
11 . . . . . . until it . . . . . . . . ..
12 . . . . . . mixture in.
13 . . . . . . in the centre of the oven for . . . . . . ..
14 . . . . . . temperature slightly for . . . . . . . ..
15 . . . . . . from the oven when the pudding is . . . . . . . ..

### Section B

### Exercise 2
The verbs in column A describe ways of preparing or cooking food.
Match them to their definitions in column B.

| A | B |
|---|---|
| 1 chop | a cook in the vapour of boiling water |
| 2 peel | b cook in a liquid so that the liquid does not boil |
| 3 boil | c cut into thin pieces of similar size |
| 4 fry | d cut roughly into smaller pieces |

| A | B |
|---|---|
| 5 roast | e remove the skin (from fruit and vegetables) |
| 6 stuff | f cook in hot liquid such as boiling water |
| 7 grill | g cook in a pan with fat or oil |
| 8 slice | h cook in dry heat in an oven |
| 9 steam | i fill (meat, vegetables, *etc.*) with mixture of food before cooking |
| 10 simmer | j cook in a strong heat that is directly above or below (*e.g.* on a barbecue) |

Now use some of these verbs (and the ones in the dialogues) to help you write out the recipe for a favourite dish.

## Exercise 3

a scald = a burn from very hot liquid or steam.
Complete these instructions on what to do if a child is scalded by hot water or other liquid. Use the verbs from the list below.

---

to take off   to cover   to call   to break   to do
to remove   to take   to put   to put   to run

---

1 Immediately . . . . . . . the scald under cold water or . . . . . . . plenty of cold water over it to reduce the heat in the skin. . . . . . . . this for at least 10 minutes. . . . . . . . any clothes covering the scald so that the water can get to it.
2 . . . . . . . anything tight like a belt or jewellery. Scalded skin can swell up.
3 Next . . . . . . . the scald with a clean, non-fluffy cloth like a clean cotton pillowcase or a linen tea towel. This cuts down the danger of infection.
4 Then . . . . . . . an ambulance or . . . . . . . the child to hospital.
5 Don't . . . . . . . butter, oil or ointment on a scald. It only has to be cleaned off again before treatment can be given. Don't . . . . . . . any blisters. You'll let germs in.

## Exercise 4

Here are examples of good table manners in Britain
Always say 'please' when you want something.
Never speak with your mouth full.

Don't wave your knife, fork or spoon in the air.
What advice would you give to a visitor to your country? Make
similar sentences about table manners at home.

## Writing

Use the language in this chapter to write instructions for making one
of your national dishes.
Compare what you have written with a version in an English language
cook book.

# CHAPTER 18

# WHAT DID SHE SAY?

## 18.1 DIALOGUES 📼

### (a) Dialogue 1

Brigitte sees Laurent in the lobby of the hotel.

*Brigitte*: Hello, Laurent? What's the matter? What's up?

*Laurent*: I'm not very happy . . .

*Brigitte*: I can see that. What's happened?

*Laurent*: I rang my mother this afternoon . . .

*Brigitte*: And . . .?

*Laurent*: Well, I'm afraid I've had some bad news . . .

*Brigitte*: Oh dear. What did she say?

*Laurent*: Well, she told me that I'd failed my baccalaureate exam . . .

*Brigitte*: Oh no! What did you say?

*Laurent*: What could I say? I said I was very sorry . . .

*Brigitte*: So what will you do?

*Laurent*: Well, I think I'll have to take it again. Anyway, I told my mother I would. She seemed quite pleased and told me not to worry because they would support me and give me another chance to pass.

*Brigitte*: So when will you go home?

*Laurent*: Well, I think I'll finish the course I'm doing and then go home at the end of August.

*Brigitte*: It must be very disappointing . . .

*Laurent*: I guess, it's part of life . . .

### (b) Dialogue 2

A little later Brigitte sees Seiki and tells him about the conversation with Laurent.

*Brigitte*: Hi, have you seen Laurent today?

*Seiki*: No, why?

*Brigitte*: He's had bad news. He's just been told that he's failed his exam . . .

*Seiki*: Oh no! How's he taking it?

*Brigitte*: As well as can be expected. He's quite upset but I asked him what he would do and he said he thought he would like to take it again.

*Seiki*: Oh well, I suppose he'll survive. He's still very young . . . Sometimes it's better not to ring home! I spoke to my family yesterday and I felt very homesick . . . Do you find the same thing?

*Brigitte*: Oh yes. Especially when my mother says she misses me. Still, I'll be home soon . . . I must say I'm looking forward to going back. I've enjoyed my stay in England but I'm beginning to miss my room and dog and my mother's cooking . . .

*Seiki*: Yes, there's no place like home . . .

## 18.2 VOCABULARY

### (a) Dialogue 1

#### (i) Useful expressions

- When someone looks sad or ill we sometimes ask:
  What's the matter?
  What's up?
  What's happened?
  Notice the intonation Brigitte uses. It shows she is interested in Laurent's problem. These expressions give the other person a chance to talk about their problem.
- I rang my mother
  = I telephoned my mother.
- I'm afraid
  is also used to introduce bad news.
  It means I'm sorry, but . . .
  Can you tell me the way to the zoo?
  I'm afraid I can't help you.
- Oh dear!
  I'm sorry to hear that.
- I failed my exam
  If you fail, you do not reach the standard necessary for a pass.
  I failed my exam. The pass mark was 50 and I only got 45.

(ii) **Words to learn**

- exam

  An official test to show your knowledge.

  Less formal than examination.

- to support someone

  When you support someone in your family, you give them money and/or help.

- to pass

  To reach the standard in an exam. Opposite of to fail.

  I can drive now; I passed my test yesterday.

## (b) Dialogue 2

### (i) Useful expressions

- How's he taking it?

  What is his reaction to the news?

  He took the news of his mother's death very badly.

- As well as can be expected

  Here as well as means in a way that is appropriate or right for the circumstances.

## 18.3 EXPLANATIONS

### (a) Direct and indirect speech

| Direct speech | Indirect speech |
|---|---|
| You've failed your exam. | She told me that I'd failed my exam. |
| I'm very sorry. | I said I was very sorry. |
| I'll take it again. | I told her I would take it again. |
| We'll support you. | She told me they would support me. |

When we want to report someone's words we can give the exact words.

She said, 'You've failed your exam.'

This is known as direct speech.

Or, we can use indirect speech (this is also known as reported speech).

She said that I'd failed my exam.

In indirect speech the tenses, word order and pronouns may be different from those in direct speech.

For example, when the reporting verb is past (she said, he told, he replied, *etc.*) the verbs in reported speech are usually further back in the past because we are not talking at the same time as the speaker was.

| Direct speech<br>**Present** | Indirect speech<br>**Past** |
|---|---|
| I like apples. | He said he liked apples. |
| I'm sorry. | She said she was sorry. |
| **Present progressive** | **Past progressive** |
| It's snowing. | She said it was snowing. |
| **Past simple** | **Past perfect** |
| I didn't know. | She said she hadn't known. |
| **Present perfect** | **Past perfect** |
| You've failed your exam. | She told me I'd failed my exam. |
| **Shall/will** | **Should/would** |
| I'll go home at the end of August. | He said he would go home at the end of August. |
| Can, may<br>Would, could, might<br>Ought, should<br>Must | Could, might<br>Would, could, might, ought<br>Should<br>Must, had to |

Exceptions:

(i) Past perfect verbs in direct speech are not changed in indirect speech.

(ii) When the reporting verb is present, future or present perfect, we usually use the same tenses as the original.
I don't want to go.
He says he doesn't want to go.

(iii) When the idea in the reported statement also applies to the time of reporting.
The world is round.        He said the world is round.

A: I'm hungry.
B: What did you say?
A: I said that I'm hungry.
B: Let's eat.

In some of the examples we have used the conjunction that after reporting verbs. In others we have not. It is often more natural not to use that in spoken language.

Orders, requests and advice in the form of the imperative (Wait!, Please come quietly, Be careful, *etc.*) are often reported with an infinitive.

The teacher told the students to stop talking.

When the order or request is negative: Don't worry!

We use the negative infinitive.

She told me not to worry.

#### (b) Reporting questions

Reported questions do not have the same word order as direct questions.

What will you do?

I asked him what he would do.

How do you feel?

The nurse asked her how she felt.

If there is no question word (What, where, how, *etc.*) we use if or whether.

Do you have any children?

He asked me if I had any children.


### 18.4 BACKGROUND

#### Education

If Laurent were English he would take 'A' levels in order to enter university. Students who take 'A' levels are usually 18+. They are less than 10% of the students who go to school.

British parents must see that their children receive efficient full-time education from the ages of 5 to 16 years. Most children attend state maintained schools. These do not charge fees. The majority of secondary schools–called comprehensive schools–accept pupils of all levels of ability, though a few go to the very small number of grammar schools which select the pupils they take.

There are also independent schools, which charge fees. These are usually known as 'public schools' and they include very famous schools, such as Harrow and Eton College. Only about 6% of children attend independent schools.

Eton College

A comprehensive School

Some important changes are being made to the education system at present, and parents in future will have more rights and more responsibility for their children's schooling. In 1988, a new examination, the General Certificate of Secondary Education (G.C.S.E.) was introduced to replace the General Certificate of Education (Ordinary Level) and the Certificate of Secondary Education. The new exam places more emphasis on practical work and marks are given for work done during the course. Another important change will be the introduction of a national curriculum. There is a national curriculum in many countries but not yet in Britain.

The education for students from 16 – 18 is also changing. There is more emphasis on technical and vocational education.

There are also plans for more students to follow suitable courses at universities and polytechnics. To follow these, students need to get satisfactory grades in the 'A' level exam. The exam is also being changed to meet the needs of a wider range of students and the needs of the country.

## 18.5 EXERCISES

### Section A

### Exercise 1
Look at the dialogues again and complete these examples of indirect speech.
a  Brigitte asked Laurent what . . . . . . was.
b  He told her . . . . . . . that afternoon and she had given him some bad news.
c  His mother told him . . . . . . . .
d  Laurent was very upset and . . . . . . . take the exam again.
e  Seiki asked Brigitte . . . . . . . it. She said . . . . . . ..

### Exercise 2
You are Laurent. Report the questions Brigitte asked you in Dialogue 1.
**She asked me what was up.**

### Exercise 3
You are Seiki. You meet Hank. Report the conversation you had with Brigitte in Dialogue 2.

### Section B

### Exercise 4

Where do you work?
Why are you here?
How long will you stay?
Where are you from?
How long have you been in England?

Yesterday Seiki was interviewed by a reporter. He is telling Brigitte about the interview. Give his words. The reporters questions are in the notebook above.
**He asked me where I worked.**

**Exercise 5**

Alice is a teacher. She often has to give people advice. What advice did she give these people. Use **advise**, **tell** or **ask**.

1 Mark is 13. He has a bad cough. He smokes 45 cigarettes a day.
2 Gina is very lazy. Her exam is in two months.
3 Peter always talks in class. He never listens to the teacher.
4 John is almost 16. He wants to leave school but he has no qualifications.
5 Mary failed her exams. The next exam is in December. She would probably pass.
6 Albert's mother worries a lot about her son. Although he is 16 she always picks him up from school.
7 Mary always speaks English during the French class.
8 Mr Potter wants to know how he can help his daughter with her maths.

**She told Mark to stop smoking.**
or
**She advised Mark to smoke less.**

**Exercise 6**

Look at the following examples of reported speech. What did the speaker say?
The woman said she often thought about her son.
**I often think about my son.**

1 She said she hadn't seen him for ages.
2 She had however just heard that he had been arrested for murder.
3 The police told her that his gun was found near the body.
4 The police asked the boy if the gun was his.
5 They also asked him for his address.
6 The man claimed that he did not have one.
7 The policeman said that he did not believe this.
8 Yesterday, a police spokesperson said they were interviewing a young man for the murder.

**Writing**

You are Hank. You are writing to your wife. Report the conversation you had with the doctor in Chapter 14. Look at Chapter 15 again to help you invent an end to the conversation.

# IF I WERE YOU . . .

## 19.1 DIALOGUES

**(a) Dialogue 1**

Laurent and Brigitte are sitting outside in a café in Mayfair. A couple comes up to join them.

*Man:* Excuse me, do you mind if we join you? I'm afraid it's rather full inside.

*Laurent:* Of course not, I'll move our things.

*Woman:* Thanks.

*Brigitte:* As I was saying, I reconfirmed my flight home this morning . . .

*Laurent:* Have you finished your shopping?

*Brigitte:* Oh yes, I've run out of money. How about you? What will you be taking back to Paris? You ought to take something.

*Laurent:* I'm not sure. I really haven't started yet. I don't know what to get.

*Brigitte:* You ought to start soon. You should get your Mum a sweater. There are some very nice ones in the shops.

*Laurent:* That's quite a good idea. Do you think you might have time to help me look for one this afternoon? I'd appreciate your help.

*Brigitte:* I might. How about your father? What will you get him?

*Laurent:* I've no idea. He's got everything!

*Brigitte:* Well, if I were you, I'd start looking for something.

*Laurent:* You're absolutely right! There has to be something you can't get in Paris that my father wants.

*Man:* I'm sorry to interrupt, but do you live in Paris?

*Laurent:* Yes . . .

*Man*: Would you mind terribly if we asked you for some advice . . .

*Laurent*: Er . . . What can I do for you?

*Woman*: Well, we're taking the car to France and would like to stop off in Paris on our way to the south . . . but we're told that the traffic is very bad. We were wondering if you could recommend a hotel where we can park.

*Laurent*: Well, most of the big hotels in Paris have underground car parks but they're not cheap and it's not easy to get in and out of the centre. If I were you, I'd stay in one of the new hotels on the ring road. We call it the Boulevard Périphérique. They're modern and comfortable and it's quite easy to park near them. Quite a few are near metro stations. In fact, you might want to try the Hotel Juniper in Pantin. It's very close to a metro station and pretty convenient for roads coming in from the north, but there are many others.

*Man*: Thank you so much for your help.

*Laurent*: How long will you be staying?

*Man*: About three days. We hope to see quite a lot!

*Brigitte*: You really should stay longer. Paris has got everything–monuments, wonderful museums, attractive architecture, really good restaurants and beautiful shops, although things are just a bit expensive.

*Laurent*: Eating out isn't.

*Brigitte*: Yes, that's true. When are you hoping to visit?

*Man*: Next month.

*Brigitte*: That should be nice. Paris will be getting back to normal after the summer. If I were you I'd . . .

## 19.2 VOCABULARY

### (a) Dialogue 1

#### (i) Useful expressions

- Do you mind if we join you?

  Polite way of asking whether you/they can sit at the same table.

- Of course not

  Strong way of saying no. In this dialogue it means that Brigitte and Laurent don't mind. The couple can sit with them.

  Do you think it's true?

  Of course not.

- As I was saying . . .

  A way of going/returning to a topic of conversation after an interruption.

- To run out of ...
  If you run out of something you have no more left.
  We often ran out of petrol during the war.
- How about you?
  Way of asking person what they think or want. We usually use this after we say what we think or prefer.
  I like tea. How about you?
  We also use How about ... to introduce a topic in a conversation.
  Yes; that's true, but how about oil? Will it run out?
- Do you think you might ...?
  Very polite request.
- I'd appreciate it
  If you say you would appreciate help or advice you mean that you would be pleased and grateful for the help and advice.
- I'm sorry to interrupt
  If you interrupt someone it means that you stop them from talking or doing something.
  I'm sorry to interrupt is a polite way of doing this.
  I'm sorry to interrupt your work but can you help me? I'm lost.
- What can I do for you?
  How can I help you?
- To stop off
  To stop for a short time in the middle of a journey.
  I stopped off in London on my way home.
- We were wondering
  Forms of to wonder if ...can be used to introduce polite requests or questions.
  I wonder if you'd mind closing the window?

(ii) **Words to learn**
- café
  A place to buy drinks and light meals or snacks.
  In the summer some fashionable cafés in London have tables outside.
- to join
  When people or things come together, they join.
- rather
  Adverb. Here it means very.
- to reconfirm
  When you reconfirm something you check it again.
- flight
  Journey by aeroplane.

- to recommend
  If you recommend something or someone you suggest it/they is/are suitable.
  I recommend him for the job.
  Can you recommend that restaurant?
- metro
  The Paris underground
- ring road
  A ring road is a road that takes traffic round a city rather than through the middle. Paris has a large ring road. The main ring road around London is the M25 motorway. (see Background, page 170)
- convenient
  Well placed. If something is convenient it saves you time and trouble.
- to eat out
  To eat in a restaurant (rather than at home).

## 19.3 EXPLANATIONS

### (a) Ought

#### (i) Form

Ought is a verb like **would, could,** *etc.*
Like **would, could,** *etc.* it has no (–ing) forms, and no (–s) in the third person singular. We say **ought to go** (not **would to go**). Ought is always followed by the infinitive with **to.**
I ought to go.
You ought to see a dentist.
Questions: Ought we to go?
Negatives: We oughtn't to stay much longer.

#### (ii) Use

We use it to remind ourselves or someone else that they have a duty to do something, or in order to give people advice.
You ought to phone your father.
You ought to walk more.
In this sense **ought to** is very similar in meaning to **should** although **ought to** is sometimes stronger.

### (b) Should

Should is often used to talk about duty and obligation and to give advice.
You should help your mother.
You should clean the kitchen.

Often it is used to express an opinion.
Britain shouldn't be a nuclear power.
It is also used in conditional sentences.
If I were you I should buy him a present.
In if sentences and in sentences with wish we often use the past for a present situation.
I wish I knew her name. (I don't)
If I had more time, I would go and see her. (I haven't got the time)

## 19.4 BACKGROUND

### (a) Tourism in Britain

Tourism is a major industry in Britain. Tourists come from all over the world. What do visitors do when they come to Britain?

75% of all visitors come to London. Some of the most popular places for sightseeing are:

The Tower of London which is where the Crown Jewels are kept.

Westminster Abbey where the kings and queens of England are crowned and where many famous people are buried.

The Houses of Parliament with the famous clock 'Big Ben' and Westminster the centre of government.

St Paul's Cathedral which was built by Christopher Wren. It is sometimes used for royal weddings. Prince Charles and Lady Diana got married there.

Trafalgar Square with Nelson's Column.

Piccadilly Circus with the statue of Eros.

Many visitors also go to the British Museum, Madame Tussaud's famous waxworks, the National Gallery, the Tate Gallery and the Science Museum.

But where do people go and what do they do outside London?

Many visitors go to Stratford-upon-Avon to visit Shakespeare's birthplace and to go and see plays in the Memorial Theatre.

Edinburgh, the capital of Scotland, is famous for its castle, its fine buildings and the annual arts festival in August.

The city of York still has a beautiful cathedral and medieval walls. York was also the home of the Vikings who came to Britain from Scandinavia over a thousand years ago. York was called Jorvik and visitors to the Jorvik Viking Centre can see, as they ride round in small, electronically-controlled cars, something of what life was like in the tenth century.

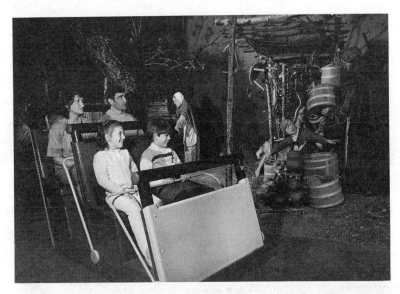

Oxford and Cambridge are popular destinations because of the famous universities, and many visitors go on tours around the Colleges.

These towns and others like Bath, Canterbury, Chester, Exeter and Norwich, all draw visitors because they have beautiful buildings and architecture, but there are many other attractive places in Britain.

### (b) Souvenirs

Many visitors to Britain spend a lot of time in shops and they buy things like sweaters, china and raincoats to take home.

Visitors also like souvenirs to remind them of their stay. The things you can buy include tea towels, key rings, flags, mugs, models and dolls.

## 19.5 **EXERCISES**

**Section A**

**Exercise 1**
Look at the dialogue in this chapter. List the advice that Brigitte has for Laurent.
Use **ought to** or **should**.
**You ought to start shopping soon.**

**Exercise 2**
Look at the dialogue in this chapter.
Use **should** or **shouldn't** to summarise the advice Laurent gave to the couple.
**You shouldn't stay in the centre.**

**Exercise 3**
What would you say in each situation?
Use **If I were you** . . .
A friend at work looks very ill.
**If I were you I'd go to see a doctor. (go home to bed, *etc.*)**
1 A colleague has a bad toothache.
2 A friend failed his driving test for the first time.
3 A visitor wants a souvenir of something that your town is famous for.
4 A friend wants to learn your language.
5 Your partner wants to get up early the next morning.
6 A good friend is getting fat.

**Section B**

**Exercise 4**
A friend is going on a beach holiday. What are the things he/she ought to take, wear and do?
**You ought to take sunglasses.**

**Exercise 5**
Somebody is coming to visit your country. What should they see and do?
Use **ought to** and **should**.

## Exercise 6

Look at these illustrations. They show what tourists should and shouldn't do to protect themselves. What advice would you give visitors to your country?

## Writing

Imagine that a friend is coming to visit your country for five days. Write a letter suggesting what he/she should see and do during the visit.

Use the following expressions in your letter.

Dear X,

I'm so glad that you are going to visit (place) in (month).

I think you should stay in (place).

You ought to see (places).

You should try to (things to do).

You must come and see us.

Looking forward to . . .

Yours,

# CHAPTER 20

# NEXT YEAR WE COULD MEET IN GERMANY

## 20.1 DIALOGUES 📼

### (a) Dialogue 1

Brigitte is at one of the check-in desks at Heathrow Airport. Margaret is waiting for her.

A check-in desk at Heathrow

*Ground hostess*:   Could I see your ticket, please?

*Brigitte*:   Here you are.

*Ground hostess*:   Smoking or non-smoking?

*Brigitte*:   Non-smoking.

*Ground hostess*:   Right, could you put your bag on the scales, please?

*Brigitte*:   Sure.

*Ground hostess*:   Have you got any hand luggage?

*Brigitte*:   Just this bag here.

*Ground hostess*:   Here's a label for your hand luggage and your boarding card. The plane will be boarding in thirty minutes. We don't expect any delays. Have a good flight!


**(b) Dialogue 2**

*Brigitte*:   Phew! I'm sorry but that took ages!

*Margaret*:   It's always very busy at this time of the year. Now, you've got time for a drink, haven't you?

*Brigitte*:   I'd love one.

*Margaret*:   Well, there's a place over there.

*Margaret*:   You managed to say goodbye to Hank and Laurent, didn't you?

*Brigitte*:   Yes, I saw them at breakfast. I think Laurent was quite sad to see me go. Anyway, we'll probably keep in touch.

*Margaret*:   I thought Laurent was very nice.

*Brigitte*:   He was. And Hank was OK, too. So, what are you up to next summer?

*Margaret*:   I'm not sure yet.

*Brigitte*:   Are you thinking of going abroad?

*Margaret*:   I might be. Why?

*Brigitte*:   Well, perhaps we could meet in Germany next year.

*Margaret*:   In Germany?

*Brigitte*:   Yes! Why not? Düsseldorf is a nice town with a really interesting old quarter and parts of the Rhine are very beautiful. Hermann and his family usually go camping on the Rhine in August, so perhaps we could hire a tent or caravan and join them for few days. We could go to Köln, I think you call it Cologne, and Koblenz where I was born and maybe down the Mosel. We'd have a great time and I'm sure Hermann and my mother would love to meet you. You will come, won't you?

*Margaret*:   I'd love to. Look, I'll ask my boss when I can take a holiday next summer and let you have some dates. There shouldn't be any problems. But are you sure you want to spend your holiday at home?

*Brigitte*:  Absolutely. So, that's settled. I shall look forward to hearing from you.

*Margaret*:  What's your flight number?

*Brigitte*:  LH 432.

*Margaret*:  I think they've just called your flight. You don't want to miss it, do you?

*Brigitte*:  You're right. I'd better go. Look, you couldn't pay the bill, could you?

*Margaret*:  Sure! Look, the departure lounge is through there. Why don't we say goodbye here?

*Brigitte*:  Well, thanks for everything. It was really good of you to bring me to the airport.

*Margaret*:  It's been a pleasure. I like seeing people off.

*Brigitte*:  I've had a wonderful time. Please send my regards to Peter and your grandmother.

*Margaret*:  I will.

*Brigitte*:  And see you in Germany. 'Bye.

*Margaret*:  'Bye.

## 20.2 VOCABULARY

### (a) Dialogue 1

#### (i) Useful expressions

● Smoking or non-smoking?

In some parts of a plane you can smoke. (The smoking compartment or section)

In other parts you can't. (The non-smoking compartment or section)

The ground hostess is asking, 'Do you want to sit in a place where passengers can smoke?'

● The plane will be boarding in thirty minutes.

To board = to get on a train, boat or aeroplane to travel somewhere.

The expression means passengers can get on the plane thirty minutes from the time of speaking.

● Have a good flight!

Many workers in restaurants, airports, hotels, *etc.* use Have a good (day, flight, trip, *etc.*) as a polite way of finishing a business conversation.

(ii) **Words to learn**
- scales
  A machine for weighing people or things.
- hand luggage
  The luggage you are allowed to carry on to a plane.
- boarding card
  A card you must have to get on a plane.
- a delay
  If a flight does not leave at the correct time there is a delay.

**(b) Dialogue 2**
(i) **Useful expressions**
- That took ages
  That took a long time.
- to manage to do something
  If you manage to do something, you succeed in doing it.
  We use this, especially when it is difficult to do something.
- To keep in touch
  When you keep in touch with someone you write, telephone or visit them regularly to exchange news.
  Keep in touch. (Write, telephone or come and see me!)
  We kept in touch for years and then he just stopped writing.
  The opposite of to keep in touch is to lose touch.
- What are you up to?
  What are you doing?
- We'd have a great time
  We'd enjoy ourselves.
  Did you have a good time at the theatre?
- To take a holiday
  In many companies in England, the holiday periods are not fixed and you take your holidays in agreement with the company you work for. (see Background Section)
- I'll let you have some dates
  I'll tell you the days when I can come.
- I shall look forward to hearing from you
  If you look forward to something you want it to happen.
  Brigitte wants to receive news from Margaret.
- To call a flight
  When you call a flight you announce that the flight is boarding and the passengers should go on board.

- To see someone off
  To go to an airport, station, *etc.* to say goodbye to someone
  who is leaving.
- Please send my regards . . .
  If you send someone your regards, you are sending friendly
  wishes.
  Please give my regards to your wife.
  With warm regards, Margaret. (at the end of a letter)

(ii) **Words to learn**

- nice
  When we like something we say it's nice.
  We use this word a lot in English.
  She's a nice person. I like her.
  Nice day, isn't it?
  He's moved into a nice house.
- abroad
  To go abroad = to go to a foreign country.
  > *A*:  Where's John these days?
  > *B*:  He lives abroad.
- old quarter
  A quarter is an area of a town. In some towns there is an **old
  quarter** where the buildings may be four to five hundred years
  old.
- camping
  camping = live or stay in a tent

- caravan
  A vehicle with beds, *etc.* where people live or spend their
  holidays.
- flight number
  A flight is a journey made by an aeroplane.
  Most flights have a number.

## 20.3 EXPLANATIONS

### Question tags
#### (i) Form

These are examples of sentences with question tags.

You've got time for a drink, haven't you?
You can come, can't you?
You don't want to miss it, do you?

We form them with:

1 the auxiliary verbs be and have
2 a modal verb (*e.g.* can)
3 the auxiliary verb do in the simple present or simple past, plus a personal pronoun.

We use do when the main verb is not be, have or a modal verb.

The sentence before the question tag is normally a statement.
Normally, if the statement is positive, the tag is negative.

| Positive | Negative |
|----------|----------|
| It's a lovely day, | isn't it? |
| She will come, | won't she? |
| He speaks English, | doesn't he? |

And normally if the statement is negative, the tag is positive.

| Negative | Positive |
|----------|----------|
| You haven't met Alan, | have you? |
| It can't get out, | can it? |
| She doesn't like him, | does she? |

After Let's the tag is shall we?
Let's go to the cinema, shall we?
After an imperative (Take . . . Don't speak . . *etc.*) the tag is will you?
Close the door, will you?
Note that the form am I not is very rare in tags. We usually say aren't I?

(ii) **Meaning**
The meaning of question tags depends on the intonation.
If the voice goes down, we are asking the person to agree with us.
Lovely day, isn't it?
If the voice goes up, it is a real question.
You haven't seen my pen, have you?
A negative sentence with a positive tag is a common way of asking for help.
You haven't got a cigarette, have you?
You couldn't pay the bill, could you?

## 20.4 BACKGROUND

### A British holiday
Where do the British go when they're on holiday? What do they do? In Victorian times, the growth of the railways meant that the middle class could go on seaside holidays to places like Blackpool and Brighton. Today the seaside resorts still have accommodation, fun-fairs and entertainment but many holiday-makers prefer to go abroad because of the sun, sea and sand.

The most popular destination is Spain. Many holiday-makers take package tours where flights, food and hotel accommodation are included in the price. They seem to like the crowds and the restaurants and bars which offer a taste of home. Some people even go to self-catering apartments and villas where they can do their own cooking. Greece, Portugal and Turkey are also popular destinations for package tourists.

France and Italy are also popular destinations but the visitors often drive there. Some camp or live in caravans, others stay in holiday homes or small hotels.

More holiday-makers are also going further, and Thailand, Egypt, the United States, Mexico and the Caribbean are becoming more popular.

For the English who do not go abroad, there are many attractions apart from the seaside and the main tourist destinations like London, Oxford, Stratford and Cambridge. There are many areas of natural beauty, South Wales, the Lake District, and the Cotswolds, which are favourites with walkers. The country cottages in the beautiful countryside of Wales, Devon, Cornwall *etc.* are all places for family holidays and camping and caravanning holidays are also becoming popular.

There are also more unusual holidays. Some people travel very slowly up and down the waterways and canals in boats and barges.

Others take activity holidays where they learn a new skill like painting or a new sport like windsurfing.

Why don't you join the British on a real English holiday? It's a great way of learning the language!

## 20.5 EXERCISES

**Section A**

**Exercise 1**
Listen to the examples of question tags in Dialogues 1 and 2 again. Does the voice go up, or down? What is the function of each example?

**Exercise 2**
Put a question tag at the end of each sentence.
You want to check that something is true.
**Brigitte is German, isn't she?**

1 Brigitte's fiancé is Hermann, . . . . . . .?
2 Margaret isn't married, . . . . . . .?
3 Brigitte had never been to England before, . . . . . . .?
4 Brigitte visited Margaret's grandmother, . . . . . . .?
5 Laurent failed his exams, . . . . . . .?
6 Hermann can speak English, . . . . . . .?
7 Hank won't stay in England, . . . . . . .?
8 Brigitte doesn't live in Koblenz any more, . . . . . . .?

**Exercise 3**
Write a sentence with a question tag for each situation.
You look out of the window. The clouds are very dark. It's going to rain.
**It's going to rain, isn't it?**
1 A friend is leaving. You want to know if she managed to say goodbye to her friend Laurent.
  You ................................................................................
2 You are looking for Hank. You want to check that Brigitte has seen him today.
  Brigitte, ..........................................................................
3 You are talking about Laurent. You think he's nice. You want people to agree with you.
  Laurent's ........................................................................
4 You are at the train station waiting for a friend. You don't know the exact time the train will arrive but the train is late. Check this.
  The train .........................................................................

**Section B**

**Exercise 4**
Margaret isn't sure of her plans for next year yet but she may go to Germany.
Make five sentences about some of the things you **may** do next year.

**Exercise 5**
Complete this conversation with appropriate question tags.
*Ron:*  It was a good film, . . . . . . .?
*Beatrice:*  Yes it was but I didn't like the cinema, . . . . . . .?
*Ron:*  Oh, why not?
*Beatrice:*  It was too warm.
*Ron:*  You could have taken your sweater off, . . . . . . .?

*Beatrice*: That was the problem. I couldn't. I had nothing on underneath. Anyway, let's go and get something to eat, .......?
*Ron*: Sure.

**Exercise 6**
Write down three or four question tags you might use:
– after a meal in a restaurant.
– after a play or musical.

**Writing**
Write a letter of thanks. After an invitation, or when someone has been kind to you, or when you receive a gift, it is polite to write a letter of thanks.
When you write the letter:
● start by thanking the person.
I am writing to thank you for . . .
Thanks for the . . .
How kind of you to (invite, send me)
I can't tell you how pleased I was . . .
● say a few words about the invitation, gift, *etc.*
I really enjoyed . . .
I had a very nice time.
The (sweater) is perfect. It fits me, *etc.*
● add one or two sentences as a conclusion.
Thanks again.
Hope to see you soon.
Imagine you are Brigitte. You are at home. Write a short note of thanks to your friend Margaret. Compare your letter with the example on page 232.

# II REFERENCE MATERIAL

# KEY TO EXERCISES

**Chapter 1**

**Section A**

**Exercise 1**
*Brigitte*:  Here you are!
*Brigitte*:  I'm from Koblenz.
*Brigitte*:  Two weeks. I'm on holiday.
*Brigitte*:  The Balmoral Hotel, London

**Exercise 2**

| | |
|---|---|
| France | French |
| United Kingdom | British |
| Greece | Greek |
| Ireland | Irish |
| Spain | Spanish |
| Portugal | Portuguese |
| Netherlands | Dutch |
| Belgium | Belgian |
| America | American |
| China | Chinese |
| India | Indian |
| Japan | Japanese |

**Exercise 3**
They have goods to declare in the red channel.
They have more than the allowance.

## Section B

### Exercise 4
a accountant
b nurse
c doctor
d pilot
e taxi-driver
f businesswoman
g engineer
h teacher
i soldier
j factory worker
k labourer
l typist

### Exercise 5
Brigitte
... holiday.
... for two weeks.
Hank
... Hank.
... on business.
... here for ...
Laurent
... student.
... English.

### Exercise 6
1 are; are
2 is; is
3 Are
4 are
5 Is
6 Is
7 isn't
8 are
9 aren't
10 is

## Chapter 2

## Section A

### Exercise 1
1 *R*: Can I help you?
  *B*: Have you got ...

2 *B*: I've got
   *R*: 's your name
   *R*: do you spell it?

3 *R*: the evening.

## Exercise 2

1 six fifty-three
  seven minutes to seven

2 minutes past five
  five thirteen

3 thirty

4 seven forty-five

## Exercise 3

1 five past three
  three oh five

2 five to seven
  six fifty-five

3 Quarter to ten
  nine forty-five

4 twenty-five past one
  one twenty-five

5 twenty past seven
  seven twenty

## Section B

## Exercise 4
Scherer
Brigitte
German
Credit card (Visa)

## Exercise 5
1. a single room
2. a double room with shower
3. a double
4. a double with bath
5. a twin with bath
6. a single with bath

**Chapter 3**

**Section A**

**Exercise 1**

The correct order is:
Excuse me, is there a bank near here?
Yes. It's next to the hotel. Go straight ahead for about three hundred yards.
The bank is on the left.
Thank you very much.

**Exercise 2**

We say:
The Tower of London
The Imperial War Museum
The Bank of England

**Section B**

**Exercise 4**

Possible answers:
1 Near the Houses of Parliament.
  Opposite the Houses of Parliament.

2 In Cannon Street.
  Near the Bank of England.

3 By the Thames.
  Near Tower Bridge.

4 Off Whitehall.
  In Whitehall.
  Near St. James' Park

**Writing**

1 Go down this road to Trafalgar Square. From Trafalgar Square you go down Whitehall. Downing Street is on your right.

2 Walk to Piccadilly Circus. When you get to Piccadilly Circus take the road to the right. That's Regent Street. Walk up Regent Street until you come to Oxford Street.

**Chapter 4**

**Section A**

**Exercise 1**

The right order is:
Can I help you?
Yes, please. I'm looking for a blouse.

Certainly. What size are you?
Fourteen.
Here's a nice one.
I'm afraid yellow doesn't suit me. Have you got a blue one?
Here, try this one on.

**Exercise 2**

*A*: I'd like to change some money.
*A*: . . . what size is this?
*A*: . . . have . . .
*B*: Here . . .
*B*: . . . like to . . . one .

**Exercise 3**

. . . am . . . I'm trying on . . .
. . . are looking for . . .
. . . is changing . . .
. . . am going . . .
. . . is buying . . .

**Section B**

**Exercise 4**

   1  many
   2  a lot of/much
   3  many/a lot of
   4  many
   5  much
   6  many/a lot of
   7  many

**Chapter 5**

**Section A**

**Exercise 1**

*A*: Can
*B*: . . . a pint . . .
*A*: . . . like . . .
*B*: . . . think . . .
*A*: . . . could . . .
*B*: . . . a little . . .

**Exercise 2**

*a* a little    *f* a few
*b* a few    *g* a little
*c* a little    *h* A few
*d* a few    *i* A little
*e* a little

## Exercise 3

Could I have the lemon meringue pie, please?
No, thanks. I'll have some ice-cream.
We'll have it later.

## Section B

## Exercise 4

chips   C
cheese   U
crisps   C
beef   U
coffee   U
steak and kidney pie   C
prawn cocktail   C
beer   U
glass of wine   C
apple   C

## Exercise 5

1 Can you help me with my bag, please?
2 Could you pass the salt, please?
3 Could you tell me the way to Trafalgar Square, please?
4 Would you bring me a glass of wine, please?
5 Can I try a red blouse, please?
6 Waiter, could I have the bill, please?
7 Could I speak to Mr Brown, please?

## Chapter 6

## Section A

## Exercise 1

1 three one double one double one
2 oh two two three (double two three) eight four two three one five
3 oh five one six seven eight one six two six
4 two four two oh three six

## Exercise 2

are; live; is; works; play; plays; speak

## Exercise 3

1 doesn't work      5 doesn't speak
2 doesn't go      6 doesn't live
3 don't play      7 doesn't see
4 don't have      8 don't speak

**Exercise 4**

1 Does Hermann play the violin?
2 Where does Margaret work?
3 How often does Margaret go to 'The Three Bells'?
4 Do you like music?
5 What time do you start work in the morning?
6 Why do they go to the pub?

**Section B**

**Exercise 5**

1 Wrong–I usually play . . .
2 Right
3 Wrong–He understands . . .
4 Right . . .
5 Wrong–I think . . .
6 Right
7 Wrong–I'm studying . . .
8 Right

**Exercise 6**

Possible questions. Interests:
What type of music do you like?
What are your hobbies?
Do you play (football, the piano, cards, *etc.*)?
Day:
What time do you get up?
Where do you work?
What do you do?
How do you get to work?
Do you have lunch?

**Chapter 7**

**Section A**

**Exercise 1**

go–went; wake–woke; sleep–slept; see–saw, leave–left; tell–told; stand–stood; eat–ate; can–could; have–had; say–said

**Exercise 2**

She visited the National Portrait Gallery.
She went round Covent Garden.
She didn't buy a present for her mum.
She didn't change money.
She didn't meet Hank for dinner.
She didn't go to the theatre.

## Exercise 3
1 Did. . . go . . .
2 . . . did . . . telephone
3 . . . did . . . meet
4 . . . did . . . see. . .
5 . . . did . . . have

## Section B

## Exercise 4
1 How many suitcases did you have?
2 Which airport did you arrive at?
3 How did you travel to London?
4 How much did the taxi cost?
5 What was the weather like?
6 What was the name of the hotel?
7 Did you have a reservation?
8 What time did you arrive at the hotel?
Brigitte's answers:
1 I had one.
2 I arrived at London Heathrow.
3 I travelled by taxi.
4 It cost £18.50.
6 The Balmoral.
7 Yes.
8 At about 6 p.m.

## Exercise 5
. . . left . . . was . . . were . . . arrived . . . caught . . . took . . . slept . . .
took . . . stopped . . . started

## Writing
This morning I got up, had breakfast and went to the tube station as usual, but it was closed, so I decided to take a taxi. I waited and waited and there weren't any around, so I decided to walk. Unfortunately, I got lost. I tried to ask the way but all the people I met were foreigners so nobody understood me. It was terrible. Anyway, I walked round and round until suddenly I saw a sign for the Haymarket. I knew the school was not far from there so I followed the sign, I got there but I was just over an hour late!

## Chapter 8

## Section A

## Exercise 1
On Tuesday, she's visiting the British Museum
and going to the theatre.

On Wednesday, she's sightseeing and shopping.
She's having dinner with Laurent and Hank.
On Thursday, she's going to Cambridge.
She's visiting the Tower of London on Friday.
On Saturday she's visiting Margaret's grandmother.

## Exercise 2

1 I'll get . . .
2 I'm meeting . . .
3 I'll go . . .
4 I'll have . . .
5 I'll go . . .
  I'll be
6 . . . is going to be . . .
  I'll think . . .

## Exercise 3

1 Shall we pay the bill . . .? (Shall we go?)
2 Shall we go to the cinema?
3 What shall I buy Laurent for his birthday?
4 Shall I pour you some tea?
5 Shall we have (dish X, the same dish)?

## Section B

## Exercise 4

1 Shall we dance?
2 How about having something to eat?
3 Shall I get your coat?
4 Would you like to come to the cinema?
5 Let me do (paint) it for you.

## Exercise 6

1 Will people live longer?
2 Will we have nuclear weapons?
3 Will America still be the richest nation?
4 Will children all speak one language?

## Writing

Dear Margaret,
What are you doing next Saturday?
If you are free why don't you come to
the Arts Theatre with me? I've got two free tickets.
We could meet outside the Arts at 8 p.m.
Please give me a ring to confirm arrangements.
I look forward to hearing from you.
Yours,

## Chapter 9

### Section A

#### Exercise 1
1 ... can get ...
2 can't get in ... could see ...
3 ... 'll come ... let
4 ... is waiting ... tell
5 ... come ... I'll give ...
6 ... 'll be ... come ...
7 ... will meet ... arrive ...
8 ... pay ... 'll pay ...

#### Exercise 2
1 We might be late for the other shows.
2 I might not have time to eat before the show starts.
3 I might not have enough money.
4 We might be late.
5 You might not understand the play.

### Section B

#### Exercise 3
1 You could go to New York and see the Empire State building.
2 You could go to Paris and see the Eiffel Tower.
3 You could go to Cairo and see the Pyramids.
4 You could go to Athens and see the Acropolis.
5 You could go to Pisa and see the Leaning Tower.
6 You could go to San Francisco and see the Golden Gate Bridge.
7 You could go to London and see Trafalgar Square.
8 You could go to Venice and see St. Mark's Square.
9 You could go to Sydney and see the Opera House.
10 You could go to China and see the Great Wall.

#### Exercise 4
1 Why don't you go to Oxford Street?
2 You could go to The British Museum.
3 Why don't you go the National Theatre?
4 Why don't you go to the Stock Exchange?
5 You could go to Buckingham Palace.
6 Why don't you go to Covent Garden?
7 Why don't you go to Piccadilly Circus?

**Chapter 10**

**Section A**

**Exercise 1**
1 ... was walking ...
2 ... was stealing ...
3 ... was leaving ...
4 ... were standing ...
5 ... was trying ...

**Exercise 2**
1 Why were you walking down Oxford Street late yesterday afternoon?
2 She was not really trying clothes on.
3 Were the security men watching the woman?
4 I was walking quickly although I was tired.
5 Were you window shopping at 4 p.m.?

**Exercise 3**
1 ... was travelling ... telephoned
2 ... was putting ... saw ...
3 ... was she wearing...
4 ... did not see ... was looking ...
5 ... stopped ...
6 ... was putting ... went ...
7 ... arrested ... was leaving ...
8 ... watched ...
9 ... telephoned ...

**Exercise 4**
1 I was selling newspapers at my stall and when the bomb exploded I called the police.
2 I was collecting tickets and when the bomb exploded I ran for help.
3 I was waiting for my cousin and when the bomb exploded I went to look for her.
4 I was buying my ticket and when the bomb exploded I got on my train.
5 We were getting off the train and when the bomb exploded we left the station as quickly as possible
6 We were having a drink in the restaurant and when the bomb exploded we did not leave our table.

**Exercise 5**
1 slowly
2 incredibly
3 well
4 fast
5 quietly
6 beautifully
7 badly
8 carefully
9 completely

## Writing

While I was walking down Oxford Steeet, I stopped to look in the window of a large store. When I looked inside, I saw a woman who was putting some perfume straight from the shelf into her bag. I went into the shop but there were so many people that I couldn't see her. So, I left and continued window shopping, but when I walked into Selfridge's, there she was! This time, she was looking at some sweaters in the fashion shop and holding them up to try with one hand but the next thing, she just grabbed a sweater from the pile and put it into her coat incredibly quickly. I couldn't believe it! So, I went to the Manager. They followed her round and a security man caught her as she was leaving the shop.

## Chapter 11

### Section A

### Exercise 1

*B:* . . . has she been . . .
*B:* . . . haven't seen . . .
    . . . have you looked . . .
*L:* . . . hasn't been . . .
*L:* . . . haven't looked . . .
*B:* . . . has just come . . .
*B:* . . . has already left . . .

### Exercise 2

1 Has she already left the hotel?
2 Have you just come in?
3 Have you eaten anything this evening?
4 Have you seen Linda Lovely in the last few minutes?
5 Have they finished their meal yet?
6 Have you had your holiday for this year?

### Exercise 3

1 yet
2 just
3 just
4 yet
5 already
6 already
7 just

### Section B

### Exercise 5

1 crossed
2 has found

3 worked
4 have done
5 went
6 has finished
7 built
8 gave . . . have lost . . .

**Exercise 6**
1 for
2 since
3 since
4 for
5 for
6 since
7 for
8 since

**Writing**
Possible answer:
This man is in his late 50's. He has thin grey hair and is becoming bald.
He has a neat grey beard and wears glasses. He has an interesting face
with lines around the eyes. He looks serious. He's wearing a jacket and
tie with a shirt and sweater. However, his clothes are not very smart.

**Chapter 12**

**Section A**

**Exercise 1**
1 had looked . . .
2 wouldn't have hurried . . .
3 wouldn't have recognized . . .
4 would have arrived . . .
5 hadn't sent . . .

**Exercise 2**
1 If she hadn't missed the train, Brigitte wouldn't have arrived late.
2 If they hadn't changed the platform, Brigitte wouldn't have missed
   the train.
3 If Margaret hadn't sent Peter a photograph, he wouldn't have been
   able to recognize Brigitte.
4 If it hadn't been too far to walk, Peter and Brigitte wouldn't have taken
   a taxi.
5 Cambridge station wouldn't have been built outside the city walls if
   the University hadn't objected.

**Exercise 3**

1 I'm sorry the train left from platform 8 but it wasn't my fault.
2 I'm afraid I forgot to bring the photographs as I was in a hurry.
3 I'm sorry I can't understand Spanish.
4 ... you weren't German. (you didn't speak German)
5 ... I just don't know what to say.

**Section B**

**Exercise 4**

| | |
|---|---|
| 1 B | 4 F |
| 2 E | 5 A |
| 3 D | 6 C |

**Exercise 5**

1 If I go to Pisa, I'll see the Leaning Tower.
2 If I go to Venice, I'll see St. Mark's Square.
3 If I go to Madrid, I'll see the Prado.
4 If I go to Amsterdam, I'll see the canals.
5 If I go to Athens, I'll see the Acropolis.

**Exercise 6**

Possible answers:
The weather would have been better if he hadn't gone in winter.
The resort would have been better if it hadn't been new.
The resort would have been better if it had been built.
The holiday would have been better if there had been water in the pool.
The holiday would have been better if he hadn't gone alone.

**Writing**

2 Field Road
London SW1 2DJ

15th May ...

R Cooper
Booksellers
6 The Crescent
Bidicombe
Devon

Dear Mr Cooper,

Thank you for your letter of 10th May. I am afraid I did not receive your letter of 3rd March. I am sorry for the delay in paying the deposit but I have been abroad. I enclose a cheque for the sum requested.

Yours sincerely,

R. James

## Chapter 13

### Section A

### Exercise 1

1 Have you ever been to China?
2 Have you read any of Shakespeare's plays?
3 Who's the most interesting person you have ever met?
4 Have you never done anything wrong?
5 Have you ever tried steak and kidney pie?
6 Have you ever heard of King's College Chapel?

### Exercise 2

1 It was purchased in 1961.
2 Yes, it was founded in the sixteenth Century.
3 No, it was finished about 100 years after his death.
4 It is being painted at the moment.
5 The building will be finished some time next year.

### Exercise 3

1 My money was stolen yesterday afternoon.
2 The college is being painted.
3 The platform was changed from 14 to 8 at the last moment.
4 The meeting room has been changed.
5 Brigitte was met at the station.
6 Twenty people were killed in the air crash.
7 Will a cure for AIDS be discovered soon?

### Exercise 4

a 6
b 1
c 4
d 9
e 8
f 7
g 2
h 5
i 3

### Exercise 5

b Dynamite was invented by Alfred Nobel.
c The telephone was invented by Alexander Bell.
d Hamlet was written by Shakespeare.
e The smallpox vaccination was discovered by Louis Pasteur.
f The gramophone was invented by Thomas Edison.
g Gunpowder was discovered by the Chinese.
h The Nutcracker Suite was composed by Tchaikovsky.
i The Mona Lisa was painted by Leonardo da Vinci.
j Bleak House was written by Charles Dickens.

**Exercise 6**

1 Who is the most popular actor in your country?
2 When is the best time to visit your country?
3 Which is the most beautiful place you've ever visited?
4 What is the most interesting book you've ever read?

## Chapter 14

### Section A

**Exercise 1**

Possible answers:
1 go to bed.
2 see a doctor.
3 rest.
4 take some medicine.
1 looking at another car.
2 take it to the garage.
3 changed your car?

**Exercise 2**

1 D
2 E
3 B
4 A
5 C

### Section B

**Exercise 3**

2 D
3 H
4 G
5 C
6 E
7 F
8 B

**Exercise 4**

1 You had better take an umbrella.
2 You had better hurry.
3 You had better not go out at night.
4 You had better take the bus.

**Exercise 5**

Possible answers:
1 You should diet.
2 You shouldn't watch so much TV.

3 You should exercise.
4 You should get a new car.
5 You should change jobs.
6 You should write a book about your journey.
7 You should become a professional.

## Chapter 15

### Section A

**Exercise 1**
1 have to/must
2 have to
3 had to
4 had to
5 has to/must
6 have to
7 must

**Exercise 2**
1 The pump must have broken down again.
2 He must have already finished.
3 Oh dear, I must have given you the wrong bill.
4 No, she must have left before I arrived.
5 No, I must have been asleep.
6 He must have lost his way.

**Exercise 3**
1 I'm afraid the hot water has stopped running.
2 Excuse me, I'm afraid there's been a mistake.
3 I'm terribly sorry I've broken the vase. Is it very expensive?
4 I'm terribly sorry; I didn't realize the seat was yours.
5 I'm ever so sorry I forgot the meeting. Could we meet next week?
6 Look, I'm sorry, but the car still isn't working. What are you going to do about it?

### Section B

**Exercise 4**
Possible answers:
1 Don't worry. I haven't been here long.
2 I'm terribly sorry, but I haven't got the book with me. I'll get you another copy.
3 Excuse me, I think you've taken my coat.
4 I bought this two days ago and I'm afraid I can't get it to work.
5 I'm terribly sorry I'm late. I left home very early but there was a bad accident on the motorway.
6 I'm terribly sorry! I've spilt a little wine on the carpet, but don't worry, I'll clean it up.

7 Excuse me, there's a queue.
8 Don't worry. It's an old suit and it's ready for a clean.
9 Please try to get here earlier.
10 Do you think we could have some service?

**Exercise 5**

Possible answers:
1 He can't have found it.
2 He can't have seen them.
3 Where can it be?
4 He must have forgotten.
5 Someone must have stolen it.
6 What can she have said?
7 You can't have done it well.

**Exercise 6**

Possible answers:
1 Never mind. I've got another copy.
2 Don't worry. We won't be needing it.
3 It doesn't matter. I always have problems with names myself.
4 Don't worry. I'm not thirsty.
5 Never mind. I'm always doing that myself.

**Writing**

A possible letter:

Your address

Date of letter

Address of shop

Dear

I bought a stereo cassette recorder at your Oxford Street Store on Saturday 30 January. I am enclosing a copy of the receipt.

When I got home I found that the radio did not work.

It is not convenient for me to return the machine to your shop and I would be grateful if you could send somebody to repair it at my home.

I look forward to hearing from you.

Yours faithfully,

(Signature)

J Jones (Print name clearly)

**Chapter 16**

**Section A**

**Exercise 1**
Possible answers:
1 used to go
2 used to milk
3 used to have/live in
4 used to look after
5 used to live with

**Exercise 2**
1 she lives in a cottage.
2 she lives in the country.
3 comes to help her.

**Exercise 3**
1 had gone
2 had finished
3 had not seen
4 had written
5 had forgotten
6 had met
7 had had

**Section B**

**Exercise 4**
2 F
3 E
4 B
5 G
6 C
7 D

**Chapter 17**

**Section A**

**Exercise 1**
1 4 oz (ounces)
2 Half a pint
3 A tsp (teaspoon) of salt
4 An egg and a tbs. (tablespoon) of melted butter
5 has no lumps.
6 Put the flour, the egg, the melted butter and half a pint of milk . . .

7 Beat . . . thick
8 Add . . .
9 Pre-heat . . . 220° C. (degrees centigrade)
10 Put . . . drippings . . .
11 Heat . . . smokes.
12 Pour the . . .
13 Bake . . . 30 minutes.
14 Lower . . . 15 minutes.
15 Remove . . . golden brown.

## Section B

### Exercise 2

1 d
2 e
3 f
4 g
5 h
6 i
7 j
8 c
9 a
10 b

### Exercise 3

1 put . . . run . . . Do . . . Remove . . .
2 Take off . . .
3 cover
4 call . . . take
5 . . . put
   . . . break . . .

## Chapter 18

## Section A

### Exercise 1

Possible answers:
a the problem
b he had rung his mother
c he had failed his baccalaureate exam.
d he wanted to
e how Laurent was taking it. She said he was taking it as well as could
   be expected.

### Exercise 3

Possible answers:
Brigitte told me that Laurent had had bad news. He had just been told

that he had failed his exam. She said he was taking it as well as could be expected but he was very upset and he would be taking the exam again.

## Section B

### Exercise 4
The reporter asked me why I was here.
He asked me how long I would stay.
He asked me where I was from.
He asked me how long I had been in England.

### Exercise 5
Possible answers:
1 She told him to stop smoking.
2 She advised Gina to work harder.
3 She told Peter to stop talking.
4 She advised him to get some qualifications.
5 She advised her to take the exam again.
6 She told her not to worry.
7 She asked Mary to stop speaking English in French classes.
8 She told him to get her a teacher.

### Exercise 6
Possible answers:
1 I haven't seen him for ages.
2 I have just heard that he has been arrested for murder.
3 His gun was found near the body.
4 Is this gun yours?
5 What is your address?
6 I don't have one.
7 I don't believe this.
8 We are interviewing a young man for murder.

### Writing
Possible answer:
I went into the doctor's room and she told me to sit down. She knew it was my first visit and said she would take my history later. She asked me what appeared to be the problem. I told her that I had developed a terrible pain in my stomach at about one o'clock the night before. She asked me what sort of pain it was, whether it was sharp or dull. I told her it had been a very sharp pain. Then she asked me how long it had lasted. I told her about twenty minutes. Next, she asked me if I still had a pain. I said it was a lot better and she said that she would have a look at me. After she had examined me, she said that she had not been able to find anything wrong and it must have been something I had eaten.

230

## Chapter 19

### Section A

#### Exercise 1
Possible answers:
1 You ought to take something back to Paris.
2 You ought to start shopping.
3 You should get your Mum a sweater.
4 You should get something for your father.

#### Exercise 2
Possible answers:
1 You should stay in one of the hotels on the ring road.
2 You should stay in the Jupiter Hotel.
3 You shouldn't park in an underground car park.
4 You should stay for more three days.

#### Exercise 3
Possible answers:
1 If I were you, I'd go to see a dentist.
2 If I were you, I'd take the test again.
3 If I were you, I'd buy . . .
4 If I were you, I'd take lessons.
5 If I were you, I'd set the alarm.
6 If I were you, I'd diet and take more exercise.

### Section B

#### Exercise 4
Possible answers:
1 You ought to wear a hat.
2 You ought to use sun oil.
3 You ought to take a book.
4 You ought to take an umbrella.
5 You ought to wear a T-shirt if the sun is hot.
6 You ought to lie on a sun bed.
7 You ought to take some good books to read.

#### Exercise 6
Possible answers:
1 You shouldn't carry money in public.
2 You should lock up your valuables.
3 You should protect your car.
4 You shouldn't leave anything in your car.

**Chapter 20**

**Section A**

**Exercise 1**
1 You've got time . . .  (Voice goes down; wants her to agree)
2 You will come . . . (Goes up; genuine question; she doesn't know the answer)
3 You don't want . . . (Goes down; she expects agreement.)

**Exercise 2**
1 . . ., isn't he?
2 . . ., is she?
3 . . ., had she?
4 . . ., didn't she
5 . . ., didn't he?
6 . . ., can't he?
7 . . ., will he?
8 . . ., does she?

**Exercise 3**
Possible answers:
1 You managed to say goodbye to Laurent, didn't you?
2 Brigitte, you haven't seen Hank today, have you?
3 Laurent's nice, isn't he?
4 The train is a bit late, isn't it?

**Section B**

**Exercise 5**
*Ron:* . . ., wasn't it?
*Bea:* . . ., did you?
*Ron:* . . ., couldn't you?
*Bea:* . . ., shall we?

**Exercise 6**
Possible answers:
Meal
Lovely meal, wasn't it?
I'm full, aren't you?
The food was terrible, wasn't it?

Play or Musical
I enjoyed it, didn't you?
Great play, wasn't it?
It was boring, wasn't it?
I like his plays, don't you?

**Writing**

Dear Margaret,

I am writing a short letter to thank you for the lovely time I had in England this summer, I really enjoyed seeing you and it was very kind of you to invite me to spend a weekend with your grandmother. I cannot tell you how pleased I was to spend some time in a real English home! I really enjoyed the lunch and I'm going to try and make Yorkshire Pudding here. I also had a very nice time with your cousin in Cambridge and I will not forget our evenings in the pub! I have told everybody about my holiday and they are very envious. Please send my regards to Peter and your grandmother.

Hermann would love to meet you and I hope to see you in Germany next summer. Please write soon.

Yours,

# ESSENTIAL VOCABULARY

## 1  DAYS OF THE WEEK
Sunday
Monday
Tuesday
Wednesday
Thursday
Friday
Saturday

## 2  THE MONTHS
January
February
March
April
May
June
July
August
September
October
November
December

## 3  THE SEASONS
Spring
Summer
Autumn
Winter

## 4  SOME COLOURS
black
blue
brown
green
grey
orange
purple
red
white
yellow

## 5  THE FAMILY
grandfather
grandmother
grandchild
father
mother
brother
sister
son
daughter
uncle
aunt
nephew
niece
cousin
grandson
granddaughter

## 6  CLOTHING
blouse
dress
ear-rings
handbag
jacket
shirt
shoes
skirt
socks
stockings
sweater
tie
trousers

## 7 PARTS OF THE BODY
head
face
eyes
mouth
neck
shoulder
chest
back
arms
elbows
hands
fingers
legs
knee
feet
toes

## 8 FOOD
meat
beef
lamb
chicken
pork
liver
fish
eggs

rice
potato
pasta

stew
grill
bake
steam
roast
fry
boil

## 9 DRINK
orange (apple, tomato,
*etc*.) juice
soft drink
tea
coffee
wine
beer
whisky

## 10 FRUIT
apple
banana
grapes
orange
peach
pear
pineapple
plum

## 11 JOBS
artist
businessman (woman)
dentist
doctor
engineer
nurse
lawyer
police officer
secretary
shop-keeper
taxi-driver
teacher
writer

## 12 SHOPS
baker
bookshop
boutique
butcher
chemist
department store
greengrocer
grocer
newsagent
supermarket

## 13 TRANSPORT
aeroplane
bicycle
bus
car
motorcycle
taxi
train
tram
underground (tube)

## 14 LANGUAGES
Arabic
Chinese
English
French
German
Hindi
Japanese
Portuguese
Russian
Spanish

## 15 SCHOOL AND UNIVERSITY
examinations
class
timetable
public school
state school
degree
college
undergraduate
graduate
postgraduate

## 16 HEALTH
ill
headache
stomach-ache
cough
cold
flu
pain

## 17 MONEY
bank
bank account
cash
cheque
cheque book
cheque card
coins
credit card
money
notes
traveller's cheque

## 18 TOURISM
coach tour
guest house
guide
guide book
hotel
map
sight-seeing
souvenir
tourist
train

## 19 HOUSE
bedroom
bathroom
dining room
garden
hall
kitchen
living room
sitting room
study
utility room
toilet

## 20 FURNITURE
armchair
bed
chair
chest of drawers
cupboard
curtain
desk
door
settee
sofa
wardrobe
window

# GRAMMAR REFERENCE

# SECTION

## CONTENTS

# 1  WORD ORDER

## 1.1  THE SENTENCE

A sentence can take four forms.
a statement – The train leaves at 8 tonight.
a question – Does the train leave at 8 tonight?
a command – Open the window.
an exclamation – What a slow train!

## 1.2  STATEMENTS

Statements can be positive or negative.
These are some examples of normal English word order in positive statements.

**(a) Subject + Verb**
The man    smiled.
I          laughed.

**(b) Subject + Verb + Object**
I      had      a good time.
He     bought   a dog.

**(c) Subject + Verb + Prepositional (or adverbial) phrase**
He     went    over the bridge.
It     was     in the room.

In negative statements we put n't or not after be, have, do (Section 10) or a modal verb (Section 11).
She isn't here.
They have not come yet.
We don't eat meat.
We can't be late.

## 1.3  QUESTIONS

In questions we put be, have, do or a modal before the subject.
Is he French?
Have you finished?
Did you see him?
Can he speak English?
We can also use question words like why, where, when, *etc.*
Why can he speak English?
Where did you see him?
When did he finish?

## 1.4 COMMANDS

The normal form for commands is the imperative (Section 8.10).
Stop!
Sit down!

## 1.5 EXCLAMATIONS

In exclamations you respond to someone or something to show surprise, pleasure, anger, *etc.*
We usually use **what** + a noun or noun phrase or **how** + an adjective or special expressions like **hey** or **You what!** – which are very colloquial.
What a surpise!
How nice!
Hey!

## 1.6 OBJECTS

The object of a verb is the word or phrase that completes the meaning of the verb. Some verbs like **make** always take objects.
There are two types of objects–direct objects and indirect objects.
The direct object is a person or thing that the verb acts on. In this example **sandwich** is a direct object.
**Subject + Verb + Object**
He     made     a sandwich.
There are also indirect objects.

| Subject | Verb | Indirect object | Direct object |
|---------|------|-----------------|---------------|
| He      | made | me              | a sandwich.   |
| She     | gave | the dog         | a bone.       |

Here, the indirect object is the person or animal that receives something. We put the indirect object before the direct object unless we use words like **for**, **to**, **on** *etc.*

| Subject | Verb | Direct object | Indirect object |
|---------|------|---------------|-----------------|
| He      | gave | a bone        | to the dog.     |
| She     | made | a sandwich    | for me.         |

The normal word order is to put the indirect object before the direct object.

## 1.7 ADVERBS

Adverbs and adverbial phrases can come at the beginning, middle or end of a sentence. (Section 6.0)
Slowly, he went over the bridge.
He went slowly over the bridge.

# 2 NOUNS AND QUANTIFIERS

## 2.1 NOUNS

Nouns tell us what something or someone is called. All of these are examples of nouns.
chair (a thing)
businessman (a job)
Margaret (the name of a person)
Cambridge (the name of a place)
strength (a quality)
swimming (an action)
The different types of nouns include proper nouns (2.2), countable nouns (2.3) and uncountable nouns (2.4).

## 2.2 PROPER NOUNS

Cambridge, The Tower of London, The Prime Minister, Margaret, Parliament, *etc.* are all examples of proper nouns.
A proper noun names a person, a place or an institution (Parliament, The Church of England).
1 Most proper nouns do not take a/the.
2 Some always take the (The BBC, The Tower of London)

## 2.3 COUNTABLE NOUNS

These nouns have:
1 A plural form
   Three chairs
2 A word like a, the, her, his, *etc.* in front of them when they are singular.
   Give me a chair.
   I put it on the table.

## 2.4 UNCOUNTABLE NOUNS

1 These nouns do not have a plural form.
   Examples
   We had rice.
   They drank the milk in the fridge.

2 We cannot use a number with an uncountable noun.
We use a countable noun (+ of)
We drank three bottles of milk.
He ate 300 grams of rice.

## 2.5 QUANTIFIERS

1 We use a lot of or lots of in positive statements with countable and uncountable nouns.
He has lots of chairs. (countable)
I drank a lot of milk. (uncountable).

**Note**: With lots of the verb is singular when there is a singular subject.
There is lots of tea.
2 Much is usually used in questions and negative statements.
It is used with uncountable and singular nouns.
How much tea did you drink?
There isn't much time.
3 Many is usually used in questions and negative statements.
It is used with countable or plural nouns.
How many chairs have you got?
There aren't many sandwiches on the table.
4 We use a few with countable nouns to talk about a small number.
I have a few chairs. (two or three)
5 We use a little with uncountable nouns to talk about a small quantity.
There's only a little milk.
6 We use some in positive sentences.
I want to change some money.
We use any in negative sentences and in questions.
I haven't got any money.
Have you got any plans?
We can use some in questions when we think the answer will be yes.
Would you like some wine?
Use some and any with both uncountable nouns (*e.g.* money, tea, coffee) and plural countable nouns (*e.g.* apples, chairs)

## 2.6 's

's or s' are used with nouns to show that something belongs to somebody (or something).
1 's is added to singular nouns.
Is this Peter's book?
It is my brother's watch.
2 's is also added to plural nouns which do not end in s.
She fights for women's rights.
They play children's games.
3 When the plural has s we put an apostrophe (') after the s.
It's a boys' school.

**Note:** Do not confuse this with the short forms of verbs like to be or to have.
Peter's got Ben's watch.

# 3 PRONOUNS

A pronoun is a word that can be used in place of a noun or noun phrase. We use pronouns like he, she, they, *etc.* when we know who or what we are talking about, so we do not need to repeat the name or the noun.

Brigitte is German. She is German.

## 3.1 PERSONAL PRONOUNS

| Subject | Object |
|---------|--------|
| I | me |
| you | you |
| he | him |
| she | her |
| it | it |
| we | us |
| they | them |

He is German. (subject)

I saw her. (object)

1 We use it for a thing or an animal.

  Sometimes people use he/she for pets.

2 Many European languages have two forms of you. English has only one.

3 We do not normally use a noun and a pronoun together.

  My friend is Japanese. Not: My friend, he is Japanese.

## 3.2 POSSESSIVE ADJECTIVES AND PRONOUNS

| Possessive adjectives | Possessive pronouns |
|-----------------------|---------------------|
| my | mine |
| your | yours |
| his | his |
| her | hers |
| its | |
| our | ours |
| their | theirs |

It's my book. It's mine.

It's your book. It's yours, *etc.*

We use possessive pronouns or adjectives to show that something belongs to somebody (or something).

## 3.3 DEMONSTRATIVES

This, that, these and those are demonstratives.
We use them for things we have talked about or things which are present.

| Singular | Plural |
|----------|--------|
| this     | these  |
| that     | those  |

We use this and these for things near the speaker.
We use that and those for things which are further away.

# 4 ARTICLES

## 4.1 THE INDEFINITE ARTICLES

A or an is the indefinite article.
They are used in front of noun groups that refer to only one thing or person.
a chair   a man
The form an is used in front of words that begin with vowels (a, e, i, o, u).
an apple   an egg   an island
or vowel sounds
an hour   an MP

## 4.2 SOME USES OF 'A/AN'

1 With singular countable nouns when we mention them for the first time.
   I live in a house.
   He saw a woman.
2 Before a singular countable noun when you are saying something about the
   whole group.
   A student must work hard. All students must work hard.
   An ostrich cannot fly. All ostriches cannot fly.
   We can also use the plural.
   Students must work hard.
3 Before a job, we always use a/an.
   He's an artist.
   I'm a doctor.
4 In some expressions of quantity.
   a lot of
   a dozen
5 In prices, speed, *etc.*
   twenty pence a kilo
   fifty kilometres an hour

6 Instead of the number one in front of numbers.
  a hundred
  a thousand
  a million
  a billion
  a quarter
7 In front of certain countable nouns when you are talking about one portion.
  Give me a coffee.
  It's a good wine.
  I'll have a whisky.
8 In front of the names of artists.
  It's a Picasso.

**Note:** We don't use a/an:
1 Before plural nouns. We often use some.
2 Before uncountable nouns. (except for examples like a coffee. See 4.2.7)
3 Before the names of meals. (except where there is an adjective)
  I have breakfast at seven.
  He gave us a good breakfast.

## 4.3 THE DEFINITE ARTICLE

The is the definite article. It is used at the start of noun groups.
The is used with singular and plural nouns.

## 4.4 SOME USES OF 'THE'

1 To refer to someone or something the hearer or reader already knows about.
  I gave him a book. The book was red.
2 When you go on to explain so the hearer or reader knows who or what you are talking about.
  I saw the man with red hair.
  It was the dog I saw.
3 When you talk about things, activities or people in everyday life.
  Turn off the water. (in the kitchen)
  It was the postman. (the one who comes to us)
  Peter's in the garden. (our garden)
  She was on the phone.
4 With a singular noun to talk about a class of things.
  The panda is in danger.
  In the first few weeks, the baby feeds every few hours.
5 With plural nouns to refer generally to people or things.
  The French love food.
6 With certain titles, place names and other names.
  The Queen
  The Tower of London
  The Soviet Union
  The Times

7  With certain words like:
   the sea   the earth   the universe   the equator
**Note:** We don't use the:
1  Before names of people or places. (except certain places. See 4.4.6)
2  Before names of meals. (unless it is a special meal)
3  Before names of games. (He plays football. NOT He plays the football.)
4  Before an uncountable noun with a general meaning.
   Milk is good for you. (milk = all milk)
   but we do say: The milk in the fridge. (specific)
5  Before work as a place of work.
   James goes to work at seven.
6  When we are talking about what we use prisons, hospitals, churches, *etc.*
   for.
   I went to hospital twice as a child.
7  With phrases of time like:
   in 1978


# 5   ADJECTIVES

An adjective is a word that gives more information about a noun or pronoun.
It comes before the noun or after **be**.
A big book
She's old.
In English, an adjective has the same form in the singular or plural:
a new book   new books
and for people or things:
he's new   it's new
Adjectives can give information about:
Quality:   a nice skirt; a lovely day
Size:   a small car; a tall man; a big house
Age:   a new book; an old woman; a young girl
Shape:   a round table; a square box
Colour:   black hair; a red sweater
Origin:   she's German; a Japanese camera
Temperature:   a cold day; a hot drink
Material:   a cotton shirt; a wooden box
Some adjectives are variable. They take adverbs (see 6.0) like:
very, much, more *etc.* in front of them.
She had a **very nice** skirt.
Other adjectives do not usually take adverbs like **very, more** *etc.* in front of
them.
She was dead. (We don't say: She was more dead.)
It is cotton.


## 5.1  ORDER OF ADJECTIVES

Sometimes we use a group of adjectives together.
a big red woollen hat
a nice blue cotton skirt
When we do this, the adjectives follow an order.

These rules may help.
1 Adjectives which are variable come before adjectives which are not.
   a big woollen hat
   a nice cotton skirt.,
2 Colour adjectives come after variable adjectives and before those which are not.
   a big red woollen hat
   a nice blue cotton shirt
3 Colour adjectives can have another adjective before them which gives more information about the colour.
   a big bright red woollen hat
   a dark blue cotton shirt
Study these examples:
An expensive Japanese camera
white cotton shirts
new round tables

## 5.2 COMPARISON OF ADJECTIVES

Sometimes we compare adjectives.
This is a nice shirt. This one is nicer.
Nicer is a comparative.
We also use superlatives.
The nicest shirt.
When we use a superlative we think something is better than the others.
Here are some more examples:

| Adjective | Comparative | Superlative |
|-----------|-------------|-------------|
| tall | taller | tallest |
| useful | more useful | most useful |
| interesting | more interesting | most interesting |

The form of the comparative and superlative follows certain rules.
1 Short adjectives of one syllable (big, small, tall, nice, etc.) take -er in the comparative (taller) and -est in the superlative (tallest).
2 Longer adjectives of three or more syllables (interesting, expensive, dangerous) take more in front of the adjective in the comparative (more interesting) and most in front of the adjective in the superlative (the most interesting).
3 Adjectives of two syllables take -er/est or more/most.
   Adjectives with two syllables which end in er/y or ly usually take er/est.
   clever    cleverer    cleverest
   lovely    lovelier    loveliest
   Adjectives with two syllables which end in ful usually take more/most
   careful    more careful    most careful
4 Some very common adjectives in English are irregular.
   bad     worse    worst
   good    better   best
   old     elder    eldest (for people only)
           older    oldest (for people and things)
   little  less     least

## 5.3 SOME STRUCTURES FOR COMPARISONS

1 as . . . as and so . . . as
   With the normal form of an adjective we use as . . . as in positive
   statements and not as or not so . . . as in negative statements to compare
   two things that are the same in some way.
   The boy is as tall as his father.
   The beer is not so good here or
   The beer is not as good here.
2 than
   With the comparative we use than.
   He is taller than his father.
   The beer is more expensive here than it is there.
3 the . . . in/of
   We can express a comparison of three or more things by the superlative
   with the . . . in/of.
   The best beer in the world
   The oldest of the books

## 6 ADVERBS

Adverbs add information to the meaning of a verb by telling us how, where
*etc.* something happens.
He speaks English fluently. (How does he speak English?)
He is having lunch here. (Where?)
Adverbs can also add information to
adjectives: very big;
other adverbs: very soon;
a whole sentence: He'll probably come.

### 6.1 ADVERBS OF MANNER (HOW?)

1 Adverbs of manner (How?)
   An adverb of manner describes a verb.
   We form most adverbs of manner by adding -ly to adjectives.
   beautiful   beautifully
   It often comes at the end of a sentence because it comes after a verb:
   We went slowly.
   He drove carefully.
   or after the object (if there is one)
   She cleaned the house quickly.
   **Note:** Normally, we never put the adverb between the verb and the object.
   Brigitte speaks English well. NOT Brigitte speaks well English.

### 6.2 ADVERBS OF PLACE (WHERE?)

These are examples of adverbs of place.
They answer the question: where?

Words: abroad, anywhere/everywhere/nowhere/somewhere, forwards/
backwards, here/there, upstairs/downstairs.
Phrases: at home; in Hong Kong; on the right
Adverbs of place come before adverbs of time (6.3) but after adverbs of
manner.

| | manner | place | time |
|---|---|---|---|
| Brigitte walked | slowly | up Oxford Street | all morning. |

## 6.3 ADVERBS OF TIME (WHEN?)

These are some examples of adverbs of time.
They tell us exactly when something happens.
tomorrow, last Sunday, at three o'clock, yesterday, on 6th November,
*etc.*
They are often at the end of a sentence.
I went there on Monday.
She's going to Cambridge tomorrow.
Some adverbs of time are not so definite as to when something happens.
afterwards, already, early, once, recently, these days, suddenly, yet, *etc.*
Again they usually come at the end of a sentence.
Brigitte visited London recently.
But they can come at the start of a sentence or before the verb.
Recently, Brigitte went to London.
She suddenly went home.
When we do this the adverb of time becomes more important.
We also use adverbs like:
ago, all day, all night, *etc.*
and phrases like:
by . . ., during . . ., for . . ., from . . ., since . . .
to answer the question. How long?
We use since with points of time (Monday, 1983, three o'clock):
and for with periods of time (half an hour, twenty minutes, two days).

## 6.4 ADVERBS OF FREQUENCY (HOW OFTEN?)

Some adverbs of frequency are very definite.
Every + month, day of week, year, *etc.*
once, twice, three times (a day, an hour, a week, *etc.)*
on + (days of week)
They can be used at the start or end of a sentence.
She visits her grandmother on Mondays.
Every Monday, she visits her grandmother.
Others give a general answer.

| | |
|---|---|
| 100% | Always |
| △ | Almost always |
| | Usually |
| | Often |
| | Sometimes, occasionally |
| | Almost never |
| 0% | Never |

They usually come in mid-position after an auxiliary verb
(be, do, have, *etc.*) and before a main verb.
He is always happy.
She usually gets up at seven.
I have never spoken German.

## 6.5 ADVERBS OF DEGREE (TO WHAT EXTENT?)

These adverbs strengthen or weaken the meaning of adjectives, adverbs and verbs.
almost, a bit, enough, rather, really, quite
They go before the words they modify.
adjective:  quite good
adverbs:  quite quickly
verbs:  I quite like it.
Note that enough goes after the word it modifies.
Laurent isn't old enough to leave home.
The quantifiers a bit, a lot, a little, much can be used as adverbs of degree.
I like tea very much.
He sings a little.

## 6.6 COMPARISON OF ADVERBS

1 If the adverb is the same as the adjective, add -er to form the comparative and -est to form the superlative.
  early  earlier  earliest.
2 If it is an adverb of manner which ends in -ly use more (+ adverb) to form the comparative and most (+ adverb) to form the superlative.
  quickly  more quickly  most quickly
3 We cannot compare adverbs like daily, hourly, *etc.* as they are very exact.
4 Some adverbs are irregular.

| | | |
|---|---|---|
| well | better | best |
| badly | worse | worst |
| far | further | furthest |
| | farther | farthest |
| little | less | least |
| much | more | most |

5 Some structures we use for comparisons.
  as . . . as
  Brigitte speaks English as well as Margaret does.
  not as/so . . . as
  He can't speak English as well as Brigitte does.
  than.
  He drove more quickly than his brother.

# 7  PREPOSITIONS

Words such as by, to, at, *etc.* are prepositions.
They express relationships between things, people, places, *etc.*

## 7.1 PREPOSITIONS OF PLACE

Prepositions of place aanswer the question: Where?
Here are some examples.

1 as a point (x)

| | | |
|---|---|---|
| to | Brigitte went to Cambridge. | →X |
| | They went to the hotel. | |
| at | She stayed at home. | ● X |
| | We waited at the door. | |
| from | He walked from the underground station. | X → |
| | She came from Leeds. | |

2        as a line( _ _ _ _ _ _ _ _ _ _ _ _ _ _ _ _ _ _ _ _ _ _ _ _ _ _ _ )

| | | |
|---|---|---|
| on | Westminster is on the river Thames. | |
| off | The car turned off the main road. | |
| across | She went across the street. | |
| along | Brigitte was walking along Oxford Street. | |

3 as a surface

| | | |
|---|---|---|
| on (to) | She put the food on the table. | |
| on | Look at the picture on the wall. | |

off      He took the picture off the wall.

across      She walked across town.

through      He looked through the window.

4 as an area

in(to)      The dog ran into the garden.

in      Margaret lives in London.

out of      She went out of London.

through      We went for a walk through the garden.

5 as a volume

into      He ran into the house.

in      The cups are in that box.

out of      She climbed out of the pool.

out of      I was out of the room.

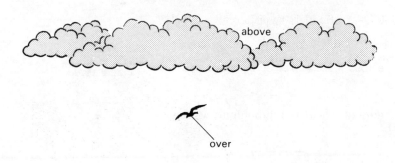

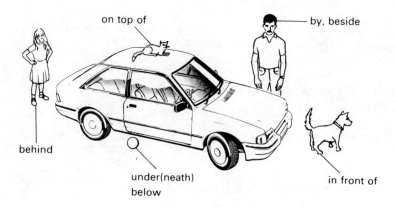

## 7.2 **POSITION**

There is a ball $^{under}_{below}$ the car.

There is a cat **on top of** the car.
A man is standing **by** the car.
There is a dog **in front of** the car.
There is a little girl **behind** the car.
A bird is flying **over** the car.
The clouds **above** are dark.

**between**

The house is **between** the two trees.

next to    opposite

The shoe shop is next to the supermarket.
His house is opposite the supermarket.

near
I live near London.

inside/outside

She's inside. He's outside.

A is at the top.
B is on the left. C is in the middle. D is on the right.
E is at the bottom.

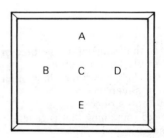

## 7.3 MOVEMENT

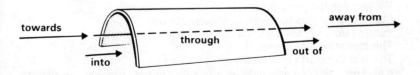

The train went towards the tunnel/into the tunnel/through the tunnel, *etc.*

up/down    He ran up and down the hill.

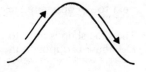

## 7.4 TIME

| at | in | on |
|---|---|---|
| at five o'clock<br>at dinner<br>at night | in August<br>in Winter<br>in 1989 | on Monday<br>on 15 August<br>on Wednesday afternoon |

# 8   VERBS AND TENSES

## 8.1 PRESENT SIMPLE

**(a) Form**
We add -s or -es to the base form of the verb in the third person singular.

I live
You live
He lives
She lives $\}$ in a house.
It lives
We live
You live
They live

**(b) Uses**
1 Something that happens all the time or repeatedly at present.
  My father works in an office.
2 It expresses habits including how often we do things.
  I get up at seven.
  We play tennis once a week.
3 It expresses something that is generally true.
  Heat rises.
4 Actions when we tell a story.
  The pub was crowded. A man walked in. She saw him. She smiles and he
  sits down.
  The sudden use of the simple present makes the story sound more
  dramatic.
  We also use the present tense in sports commentary.
  Maradona passes to Alvarez. Alvarez shoots.
5 Future reference when we refer to timetables or events.
  The bus leaves at seven.
  The festival starts in a week.
We also use the present simple for verbs like to bet, to know, to like, to
love, to hate, *etc.*
I bet you it's true.
I love you.

## 8.2 PRESENT CONTINUOUS

### (a) Form
The present continuous is formed with the present of **be** + (-ing).

| I am | | | I'm | | |
|------|---|---|-----|---|---|
| You are | | | You're | | |
| He is | | | He's | | |
| She is | waiting | | She's | waiting | |
| It is | running | | It's | running | |
| We are | | | We're | | |
| You are | | | You're | | |
| They are | | | They're | | |

### (b) Uses
1 Something that is happening at the moment of speaking
  **What are you doing?   I'm making the coffee.**
2 Something that is happening round the time of speaking.
  These situations are usually temporary but may not be happening at the
  moment of speaking.
  **What's Laurent doing these days?**
  **He's studying English in England.**
3 Talking about changes and trends.
  **Prices are rising all the time.**
  **People are smoking less these days.**
4 Planned actions in the future.
  **We're going to Germany next summer.**
  **He's arriving tomorrow morning.**
  The time expression and the context give it the future meaning.
5 We can also use the present continuous when telling a story or making a
  commentary.
  **I'm walking along when this man says to me . . .**
  **The Queen is getting out of her carriage.**

## 8.3 THE PAST SIMPLE

### (a) Form
The form of the regular and irregular past is the same for all persons.
The regular past always ends in -d.

| I walked | |
|----------|---|
| You walked | |
| He walked | |
| She walked | |
| It walked | into the room. |
| We walked | |
| You walked | |
| they walked | |

The past form of irregular verbs cannot be predicted.
**buy-bought; shut-shut; sit-sat,** *etc.*
There is a list of irregular verbs on page 268.

**(b) Uses**

1 Completed actions
   It is used to talk about past actions, situations and events, which are now finished.
   He phoned me a minute ago.
   He visited me last week.
   The Vikings went to York in 948 A.D.
2 Past habit
   I smoked twenty cigarettes a day.
   As a child, I read in bed.


## 8.4 THE PAST CONTINUOUS

**(a) Form**
The past continuous is formed with the past of be + (-ing).

I was
You were
He was
She was
It was } watching television.
We were
You were
They were

**(b) Uses**

1 Something that was already happening in the past. Often we do not know if the action is complete.
   If didn't see her: I was living in Spain in 1988.
   She was working in the office yesterday.
2 For actions which began before something else happened.
   We use the past simple for an action or short event.
   We use the past continuous for an action in progress.
   She was walking down the street, when she saw a thief.
   Brigitte met Laurent while she was living in the Balmoral Hotel.
3 To emphasise that two things were happening at the same time.
   While I was watching television, she was reading.


## 8.5 THE PRESENT PERFECT

**(a) Form**
The present perfect is formed with the present of have + (past participle).
For regular verbs the past participle has the same form as the past simple:

arrive-arrived; walk-walked, *etc.* There is a list of irregular past participles
on page 268.

| | | |
|---|---|---|
| I have | (I've) | |
| You have | (You've) | |
| He has | (He's) | |
| She has | (She's) | arrived. |
| It has | (It's) | |
| We have | (We've) | |
| You have | (You've) | |
| They have | (They've) | |

**(b) Uses**
1 When there is a connection between the past and the present.
   He's lived here for years. (He's still here)
   I've been a teacher since 1978. (I still am)
2 When past events have present importance.
   He's just arrived.
   I've finished.
Remember the present perfect is not an alternative to the past.

## 8.6 THE PAST PERFECT

**(a) Form**
The past perfect is formed with had+ (the past participle).

| | | |
|---|---|---|
| I had | (I'd) | |
| You had | (You'd) | |
| He had | (He's) | |
| She had | (She'd) | finished. |
| It had | (It'd) | |
| We had | (We'd) | |
| You had | (You'd) | |
| They had | (They'd) | |

**(b) Uses**
1 To talk about events that had already happened in the past.
   For example: There was a robbery. The thieves escaped and then the
   police arrived. We can say:
   The thieves had escaped when the police arrived.
   The past perfect makes it clear that the departure of the thieves was before
   the arrival of the police.
   Other examples:
   I got to university a year after I had left school.
   We cleaned the house when they had left.
2 As the past of the present perfect.
   By 1983 I had lived there for three years.

## 8.7 FUTURE SIMPLE

### (a) Form
The future simple is formed by **will** + (the infinitve) of the verb.

| | | |
|---|---|---|
| I will | (I'll) | |
| You will | (You'll) | |
| He will | (He'll) | |
| She will | (She'll) | go. |
| We will | (We'll) | |
| You will | (You'll) | |
| They will | (They'll) | |

The negative form is: I will not go.
The short forms are: I'll not go or I won't go.
We can also use **shall**. It does not contract in writing.

### (b) Uses
1 Will/shall can be used to say what we think will happen. (to predict events)
  I think it will rain tomorrow.
  So, I shall see you next week.
  We can also ask people to predict the future.
  Do you think it will rain?
  Will Liverpool win the match?

2 With verbs like to be sure, to hope, to think, *etc.*
  I hope she'll pass her exams.
  I'm sure they'll come here tonight.
Remember English has other ways of expressing the future.

| | |
|---|---|
| The present continuous: | The train is leaving in half an hour. |
| Be going to: | The train is going to leave tomorrow. |
| The present simple: | The train leaves tomorrow. |

## 8.8 'GOING TO' FUTURE

### (a) Form
The 'going to' future is formed by **am/is/are going to** + (the infinitive) of the verb.

| | |
|---|---|
| I am | |
| You are | |
| He is | |
| She is | |
| It is | going to leave tomorrow. |
| We are | |
| You are | |
| They are | |

### (b) Uses
1 For intentions and plans
We use this for people's intentions. Things they have already decided to do.
**I'm going to play football this afternoon.**
When we make a decision at the moment of speaking, we use **will**.
**Just a minute, I'll switch off the television.** (I'll = I will)

2 For prediction
We use it to make predictions when there is something in the present which tells us about the future. Often it is in the near future.
**Look, it's going to rain.** (There are lots of black clouds).
**Oh no, he's going to fall.**

## 8.9 USED TO

**(a) Form**
It occurs only in the past simple. It consists of **used to + (the infinitive)** of the verb in all persons.

I
You
He
She
It        } **used to sleep** in this room.
We
You
They

**(b) Uses**
1 It is used to describe something that often happened in the past but does not happen now (past habit).
**I used to smoke but I don't any more.**
**As a child I used to live in London.**

## 8.10 IMPERATIVES

**(a) Form**
The imperative form is the same as the infinitive of the verb.
**Stop!**
The negative is **don't + (the base form)**.
**Don't stop!**
For emphasis we use **do**.
**Do stop soon!**
We use the same form for any number of people.

**(b) Uses**
1 Commands, orders or requests
   **Stand up!**
   **Come here!**
   **Give me a beer, please.**
2 Warnings
   **Be careful!**
3 Invitations
   **Come and see us next week.**
4 Offers
   **Do have another drink.**
5 Instructions
   **Cook the meat for twenty minutes . . .**

6 Advice
  Always cover your head.
  Don't sit in the sun for too long.
Be careful with the stress and intonation you use. The wrong intonation can turn a request into an order.

## 9.0 THE PASSIVE

### (a) Form
The passive is formed by a tense of be + (the past participle).
Example of past simple.

|  | Subject | Verb | Object |  |
|---|---|---|---|---|
| Active | John | baked | a cake | yesterday. |
| Passive | The cake | was baked |  | yesterday. |

The object of the active verb becomes the subject of the passive verb.

### (b) Uses
1 When the person (or thing) that did something is not so important.
  The Eiffel Tower was built in the nineteenth century.
2 When the person (or thing) that did something is not known.
  His money was stolen.
3 To avoid vague subjects such as someone, or a person.
  I was asked for my name.
4 With by + (agent)
  The agent is the doer or subject of the active verb.
  We use this construction when we want to say who or what is responsible.
  Active
  Turner painted the picture.
  The storm destroyed the trees.
  Passive
  The picture was painted by Turner.
  The trees were destroyed by a storm.
The passive is often used in scientific writing and reports.

## 10  BE, HAVE, DO

Be, have, do can be used as full verbs or auxiliary (helping) verbs.

## 10.1 FULL VERBS

Be is a full verb when it combines with adjectives and nouns.
I am hungry.
He was angry.
It is Monday.
Have is a full verb when it means 'possess'.
I have a pen.

He had a car once.
Do is a full verb when it means to perform an action.
What were you doing.
I did my homework.

## 10.2 AUXILIARY VERBS

1 We use be and have to form tenses.
  For example:
  Be +(ing) for continuous forms
  I'm playing.
  He was working.
  Have + (past participle) for present perfects
  He has finished for today.
2 In the negative form we use be, have, do (or a modal verb) + n't/not.
  He isn't here.
  I have not finished.
  I don't play football.
  I didn't go last night.
  I can't stop now.
3 In questions we use be, have, do (or a modal verb) before the subject.
  Is he here?
  Have you finished yet?
  Do you play football?
  Did you go last night?
  Can you stop now?
**Note:** We use do with the present simple or past simple. These are the only
tenses that do not need be and have.
4 In short answers
  Have you finished yet?
  Yes, I have.
  Does he play football?
  No, he doesn't.
5 In question tags
  He plays football, doesn't he?
  He isn't French, is he?
6 Do is used to give emphasis.
  I do like chocolate.

## 10.3 THERE + (BE)

**(a) Form**
If the noun after there + (be) is plural, then the verb is plural.
There is a book on the table.
There are some books on the table.

**(b) Use**
We use the form when we are talking or asking about the existence of people
or things.
There is butter on the table.
Is there any jam?

## 10.4 HAVE GOT

When have got is used to mean 'to possess' it is interchangeable with the full verb have.
It is usually used only in the present tense.
I have got a new car.
Have you got a pen?
He's got black hair.
I've got two brothers.
Has he got flu?

# 11 MODALS

Verbs like can, must, may, *etc.* are called modals.

**(a) Form**
In general, modals have the same form.
There is no -s ending, -ing form, *etc.*
I must, We can, They may, *etc.*
They have not or n't after them in the negative.
We can't, I may not, You must not.
Modals function as auxiliaries or helping words in questions. The modal comes before the subject.
Can you play football?

**(b) Uses**
1 They express meanings such as someone's ability to do an action (she can sing), an action that is necessary (He must go!) *etc.*
2 Some modals can also be used to express the degree of certainty a speaker/writer feels. If we say He might be French we are very uncertain. If we say He must be French we are almost certain.

## 11.1 CAN/COULD: ABILITY

**(a) Form**

| Present | can |
|---------|-----|
| Past | could<br>was/were able to |
| Future | will be able to |

**(b) Uses**
Can and could express ability.
I can play the piano.
Can you run for twenty minutes without stopping. } Present
I couldn't spell as a child. Past
In two years the baby will be able to talk. Future
We also use was able to in the past.
As a boy I was able to run for twenty minutes without stopping.

## 11.2 CAN/COULD/MAY: PERMISSION

**(a) Form**
Present   can, could, may
We can use can, could and may to ask for permission.

Can ⎫
Could ⎬ I borrow your car?
May ⎭

Can is the most informal. It is very common in spoken English.
Could is more polite than can.
May is more formal and polite than can.
Can, may and be allowed to are also used to talk about permission.
Present   Can/may,is/are allowed to
Past      was/were allowed to
Future    will be allowed to
People can/may/are allowed to/vote at the age of 18.
As a child I was allowed to sit at the table with the adults.

## 11.3 MUST, HAVE TO: OBLIGATION

**(a) Form**

| Present | must      have to |
|---------|-------------------|
| Past    | had to            |
| Future  | will have to      |

**(b) Uses**
1 Must is used to give strong advice or orders (sometimes to oneself).
  I must stop eating.
2 Must + (the infinitive) means that something is necessary.
  It's late. You must leave.
  You must feed animals regularly.
  You must + (not or n't) + (the infinitive) means you should *not* do
  something.
  You mustn't smoke in here.
  You can use have to instead of must in present, past and future.
  I have to go.
  I had to work on Sunday.
  When you use have to in the present there is a sense that the obligation is
  external.
  When we don't have to do something it means it is not necessary for us to
  do it.
  When we mustn't do something it means it is not allowed.
  When we give advice or orders, we can choose between forms such as:
  Must = strong necessity and obligation
  Should and ought to (11.7 ) = it is advisable (in the opinion of speaker)

## 11.4 **MUST BE: DEDUCTION**

**(a) Form**
Present must be (positive only)
In the interrogative and negative we use can't be.

**(b) Uses**
1 We use it when we are sure that something is true because it is logically
necessary (we have evidence).
He must be the thief. Those are his fingerprints.
It must be mine. My name is on it.
The form must have been is used for deductions about the past.
He must have been here. That's his bag.

## 11.5 **MAY, MIGHT: POSSIBILITY**

**(a) Form**

| Present | may, might |
|---------|------------|
| Future  | may, might |

**(b) Use**
1 To express possibility.
When we use may and might there is usually some uncertainty.
The money may be/might be here.
We might go tomorrow.

## 11.6 **COULD: POSSIBILITY**

**(a) Form**

| Present | could |
|---------|-------|
| Future  | could |

**(b) Use**
1 To express possibility (especially about future actions)
It could be you.
We could go to the cinema tomorrow, couldn't we?

## 11.7 **SHOULD, OUGHT TO: ADVICE, OBLIGATION**

**(a) Form**
Present should, ought to
We should go.
When we add 'time words' they can refer to the future.
We should leave tomorrow.

**(b) Use**
To express weak obligation and give advice.
You should eat less.
I shouldn't speak to him.
You ought to vote.
Ought to is a little stronger than should.

## 12 CONDITIONALS

There are three main types: Type 1, Type 2, Type 3.

### 12.1 TYPE 1

if + (present) + (future)
If she leaves now, she will catch the train.
If I pass my exam, I'll go to university.
We use Type 1 when we think that there is a real possibility that something will happen.
Although the reference is to the future we use a form of the present tense in the 'if' part of the sentence.
We can also use modals such as can, may/might, ought to/should/must to replace the future tense.
If he works hard, he can pass his exam.

### 12.2 TYPE 2

if + (past simple) + would, could, *etc.*
If I had the money, I'd buy a new house.
If you took the plane, you'd get there earlier.
We use Type 2 to talk about imaginary future situations and the imaginary consequences. The situation is possible, but unlikely.
Sometimes, the choice between Type 1 and Type 2 depends on the speaker's attitude.
If you took the plane, you'd get there earlier. is less certain than
If you take the plane you will get there earlier.
We often use were in place of was after I/he/she/it.
The meaning is the same but it is more formal.
We usually use were when the situation is imaginary.
If I were the Queen, I wouldn't live in Buckingham Palace.
We can replace would with could, may, might, *etc.*
They make the result more unlikely.
If he worked hard, he might pass.

### 12.3 TYPE 3

if + (past perfect) + would have, could have, might have, *etc.*
If it had snowed, nobody would have come.
If Ataturk hadn't been born, Turkey would be a different place today.

We use Type 3 to talk about the imagined consequences of past situations that did not happen.

**If it had snowed** means it did not snow.

**If Ataturk hadn't been born** means Ataturk was born.

Because the consequence cannot now happen, Type 3 is the 'hypothetical' condition.

## 13   DIRECT AND INDIRECT SPEECH

We use the term 'direct speech' to describe the way we represent the spoken language in writing.

Actual spoken statement:   **'You've failed your exam.'**

We use 'indirect (reported) speech' when we are telling another person what a person says or said.

**She told me that I'd failed my exam.**

To do this we use a reporting verb. The most common reporting verbs are **say** and **tell**.

## 13.1 REPORTING VERBS IN THE PRESENT

When the 'reporting' verb is present we usually use the same tenses as the original.

**I don't want to go.**

**He says he doesn't want to go.**

## 13.2 REPORTING VERBS IN THE PAST

When the reporting verb is past (**she said, he told me, he replied**, *etc.*) the verbs in reported speech are usually further back in the past because we are not talking at the same time as the speaker was.

| Direct speech | Indirect speech |
|---|---|
| Present<br>I like apples.<br>I'm sorry. | Past<br>He said he liked apples.<br>She said she was sorry. |
| Present progressive<br>It's snowing. | Past progressive<br>She said it was snowing. |
| Past simple<br>I didn't know. | Past perfect<br>She said she hadn't known. |
| Present perfect<br>You've failed your exam. | Past perfect<br>She told me I'd failed my exam. |

| Direct speech | Indirect speech |
|---|---|
| Shall/will<br>I'll go home at the end of August. | Should/would<br>He said he would go home at the end of August. |
| Can/may<br>Would, could, might<br>Ought, should<br>Must | Could/might<br>Would, could, might, ought<br>Should<br>Must, had to |

**Exceptions**

1 Past perfect verbs in direct speech are not changed in indirect speech.
2 When the idea in the reported statement also applies to the time of reporting.

The world is round.      He said the world is round.
*A*: I'm hungry.
*B*: What did you say?
*A*: I said that I'm hungry.
*B*: Let's eat.

## 13.3 REPORTING ORDERS, REQUESTS AND ADVICE

Orders, requests and advice in the form of the imperative (Wait!, Please come quietly, Be careful, *etc.*) are often reported with an infinitive.

| Direct | Indirect |
|---|---|
| The teacher said, 'Be quiet!' | The teacher told the students to be quiet. |

When the order or request is negative (Don't worry!), we use the negative infinitive.

| Direct | Indirect |
|---|---|
| Don't worry, she said. | She told me not to worry. |

## 13.4 REPORTED QUESTIONS

Reported questions do not have the same word order as direct questions.
What will you do?'
I asked him what he would do.
'How do you feel?'
The nurse asked her how she felt.
If there is no question word (what, where, how, *etc.*) we use if or whether.
'Do you have any children?'
He asked me if I had any children.

## 14 IRREGULAR VERBS

| Infinitive | Past Tense | Past Participle |
|---|---|---|
| be | was | been |
| beat | beat | beaten |
| become | became | become |
| begin | began | begun |
| bite | bit | bitten |
| break | broke | broken |
| bring | brought | brought |
| build | built | built |
| buy | bought | bought |
| catch | caught | caught |
| choose | chose | chosen |
| come | came | come |
| cost | cost | cost |
| cut | cut | cut |
| do | did | done |
| draw | drew | drawn |
| dream | dreamt | dreamt |
| drink | drank | drunk |
| eat | ate | eaten |
| fall | fell | fallen |
| feed | fed | fed |
| fight | fought | fought |
| find | found | found |
| forget | forgot | forgotten |
| get | got | got |
| give | gave | given |
| go | went | gone |
| have | had | had |
| hear | heard | heard |
| hit | hit | hit |
| hurt | hurt | hurt |
| keep | kept | kept |
| know | knew | known |
| learn | learnt | learnt |
| leave | left | left |
| lend | lent | lent |
| let | let | let |
| light | lit | lit |
| lose | lost | lost |
| make | made | made |
| mean | meant | meant |
| meet | met | met |
| put | put | put |
| read | read | read |
| ring | rang | rung |
| run | ran | run |
| say | said | said |
| see | saw | seen |
| sell | sold | sold |

| Infinitive | Past Tense | Past Participle |
|---|---|---|
| send | sent | sent |
| set | set | set |
| shake | shook | shaken |
| shine | shone | shone |
| shoot | shot | shot |
| shut | shut | shut |
| sing | sang | sung |
| sink | sank | sunk |
| sit | sat | sat |
| sleep | slept | slept |
| smell | smelt | smelt |
| speak | spoke | spoken |
| spend | spent | spent |
| stand | stood | stood |
| steal | stole | stolen |
| swim | swam | swum |
| take | took | taken |
| teach | taught | taught |
| tell | told | told |
| think | thought | thought |
| understand | understood | understood |
| wake | woke | woken |
| wear | worn | worn |
| write | wrote | written |

# GUIDE TO PRONUNCIATION

## 1 INTRODUCTION 📼

In learning a foreign language it is important to pronounce words and sentences so that others understand you. This guide can help you.

The pronunciation in this section is standard British English which is understood by many speakers of English all over the world.

Good pronunciation comes from listening and imitating.

So read, listen and try to copy the examples on the cassette that comes with this course.

To help you follow the pronunciation guide we have used symbols from the International Phonetic Alphabet.

**Remember**

- A number of sounds in English may be new to you, because they are not in your language.

  For example, do you have these sounds in your language?

  tʃ     ʃ     θ

- The pronunciation of some words change when they are joined with other words in a sentence.

  Listen to how we say

  **What are you doing at the weekend?**

  or

  **I went last year.**

- The 'stress and rhythm' of English sentences may be different from sentences in your own language. (see Section 3)

- The meaning of sentences in English may change with the 'intonation'. (see section 4)

- English spelling may not help.

  Notice how these words are usually pronounced:

  **laugh   because   woman**

## 2  THE SOUNDS 📼

### (a) Vowels
i:    me, green, cream
ɪ     fit, list, fish
ɛ     bed, red, said
æ     man, map, bag
ʌ     but, must, come
ɑ:    start, card, far
ɒ     dog, top, shop
ɔ:    talk, thought, form
ʊ     wood, cook, look
u:    you, use, choose
ɜ:    her, shirt, turn
ə     a, banana, camera

### (b) Diphthongs
eɪ    play, say, steak
aɪ    eye, guide, pint
ɔɪ    boy, boil, enjoy
əʊ    goat, coat, road
aʊ    out, down, loud
ɪə    clear, beer, near
eə    wear, hair, fair
ʊə    sure, poor, cure

### (c) Consonants
b     bed, baby, Rob
d     done, dreadful, hand
f     fit, self, laugh
g     good, luggage, dog
h     hat, hot, high
j     yellow, you, beautiful
k     kind, likes, cook
l     love, slim, lovely
m     mat, member, form
n     nine, Sunday, again
p     pay, people, top
r     run, trouble, really
s     soon, sisters, thanks
t     talk, stand, toast
v     very, never, leave
w     would, sweet, window
z     zoo, lazy, visit, blouse
ʃ     show, finished, fish
ʒ     measure, usually
ŋ     sing, finger
tʃ    cheap, researcher, watch
θ     thin, something, month
ð     then, that, mother
dʒ    joy, passenger

# 3 STRESS 📼

The rhythm of English comes from the correct placing of stress within a word and within a sentence.
The word **be** is one syllable.
The word **believe** is two syllables.
The word **believable** is four syllables.
Within a word there is heavy stress on one syllable. This is 'word stress'.
Within a sentence the important words carry the heavy stress. This is 'sentence stress'.

## 3.1 WORD STRESS

Listen to the examples of word stress.
Repeat them.

| | | |
|---|---|---|
| certain | terrible | interest |
| certainly | terribly | interesting |
| difficult | possible | embarrass |
| difficulty | possibility | embarrassing |

It is important to learn and practise where the stress falls in each new word you learn.

## 3.2 SENTENCE STRESS 📼

Now listen to the examples of sentence stress.

How many times have you been there?

Three times.
Repeat the sentences. Note how the strongly stressed words carry the meaning.
The words in between are spoken rapidly and have weak stress.
Note the stress in the following examples.
I want to.
I want to go.
I want to go now.
I want to go tomorrow.
Mary and George want to go tomorrow.
The stress words come at roughly regular intervals.
'Rhythm' is the regular repetition of stress in time.
English is said to have a 'stress-timed rhythm' because the stressed words come at regular intervals. Therefore the following sentences of different lengths take the same number of seconds to say because they contain two stressed words: lost and shirt.
1 I lost my shirt.
2 It's my shirt I lost.
3 But it's my shirt that I lost.

A language like Spanish is 'syllable timed'. Each syllable takes the same time to say. In Spanish, a sentence of seven syllables will be much longer than a four-syllabled one.

Is your language syllable timed?

## 3.3 WEAK FORMS 📼

To make it possible for the stressed words to come at regular intervals in the sentence, some words have a weak (unstressed) form which is used when the word is not important.

In unstressed syllables the vowels often become the weak unstressed vowel sound / ə/. This sound is the most common sound in spoken English.

Listen to these examples.

|  | strong | | weak | |
|---|---|---|---|---|
| a | eɪ | (unusual) | ə | |
| am | æm | | əm | |
| an | æn | (unusual) | ən | |
| and | ænd | | ənd, | ən |
| are | ɑː (r) | | ə (r) | |
| at | æt | | ət | |
| been | biːn | | bɪn | |
| but | bʌt | | bət | |
| can | kæn | | kən | |
| could | kʊd | | kəd | |
| do | duː | | də | |
| does | dʌz | | dəz | |
| had | hæd | | həd, | əd |
| had | hæd | | James had already gone. | |
| has | hæz | | My grandmother has gone to the shops. | |
| he | hiː | | What did he say? | |
| her | hɜː | | Do you like her? | |
| him | hɪm | | Ask him to come. | |
| his | hɪz | | What's his name? | |
| is | ɪz | | The train's on platform 14. | |
| must | mʌst | | I must go. | |
| not | nɒt | | She isn't here. | |
| of | ɒv | | Of course I can. | |
| shall | ʃæl | | What shall I do? | |
| should | ʃʊd | | You should see her. | |
| that | ðæt | | She told him that he'd . . . | |
| the | ðiː | | The door was locked. | |
| to | tuː | | She went to London. | |
| was | wɒz | | He was angry. | |
| we | wiː | | We went later. | |
| were | wɜː | | They were late. | |
| would | wʊd | | What would you like? | |
| will | wɪl | | I'll see you tomorrow. | |
| you | juː | | How do you do? | |
| your | jɔː | | Thank you for your letter. | |

Practise saying each example in its strong and weak form.

The correct use of weak forms will help you to sound English.

## 3.4 CONTRACTIONS 📼

Sometimes the weak form is shortened and linked to the word before it in the sentence.
For example:
**I'm, he'll**
These are known as contractions. Again, their correct use is very important if you want to get the stress and rhythm of English right.
Listen to these examples and repeat them.
**My brother's in Germany.**
**Do you have a lot of luggage?**
**I'm sorry I'm very busy now.**
**Excuse me, I'd like to change some traveller's cheques.**
**I'm going to Cambridge.**
**We've been here for three years.**
There are many more examples on the cassette for the Course.
Listen and imitate them.

## 4 INTONATION 📼

In addition to stress, the voice goes up and down in a sentence or series of sentences.
This movement of the voice gives extra meaning. We call it 'intonation'.
Intonation is very important. Intonation can make the sentence:
**He lives in London**
a statement or a question. Listen:
**He lives in London.** (statement)
**He lives in London?** (question)
Descriptions of intonation can be very complicated.
Here are four very common intonation patterns.
1  High fall: statements and questions with question words
   **When did she come?**
   **She came yesterday.**
   **What's his name?**
   **His name's Hank.**
2  High rise: questions for repetition or clarification
   **He's French. Is he?**
   **Really?**
3  Low rise: yes/no questions
   **Are you coming?**
   **Does he want to?**
4  Fall rise: politely correcting
   **It wasn't her car.**
   **Can you?**
   At this level it is important to listen and imitate the intonation patterns on the cassette.

# 5  PITCH 📼

Intonation indicates how the voice moves up and down.
We also make the voice louder or softer.
Pitch describes the change in how loud or soft the voice is.
Listen to these examples.
**Come here!** (angrily)
**Come here!** (quietly)
**Come here!** (invitingly)
The difference in pitch in these examples tells us something about the speaker's mood and attitude.

## 6  FILLERS AND HESITATION DEVICES

If you listen to native speakers you will hear them use:
1 Noises like **erm, mmm,** and **err.**
2 Phrases such as **you see, you know, you know what I mean,** *etc.*
These give them time to think and make them sound more natural. Listen to native speakers talking naturally and see if you can hear them. Some speakers overuse expressions like **you know** so don't follow their example. However, don't worry if you hesitate a little when you are looking for the right word. Everyone does. If you use noises like **erm, mmm** then you will sound English.

## 7  THE ALPHABET 📼

There are 26 letters in the English alphabet. Listen to how the letters are pronounced.

| | | | | | | |
|----|----|----|----|----|----|----|
| Aa | Ee | Ii | Mm | Qq | Uu | Yy |
| Bb | Ff | Jj | Nn | Rr | Vv | Zz |
| Cc | Gg | Kk | Oo | Ss | Ww | |
| Dd | Hh | Ll | Pp | Tt | Xx | |

# BIBLIOGRAPHY AND
# SOURCES OF INFORMATION

## 1  GRAMMARS

J Eastwood and R Mackin, *A Basic English Grammar* (OUP.)
(A simple introduction to grammar for students up to intermediate level.
There are bi-lingual editions in Greek, Italian and Spanish.)
A J Thompson and A V Martinet, *A Practical English Grammar* (OUP.)
(A very popular and widely used EFL grammar. Intermediate level.)
L G Alexander, *Longman English Grammar* (Longman.)
(A new upper-intermediate to advanced grammar.)

## 2  GRAMMAR REFERENCE

M Swan, *Basic English Usage* (OUP.)
(Deals with problems likely to cause difficulty in areas such as grammar,
usage, vocabulary, idioms, etc. Pre-Intermediate to intermediate.)
R Murphy, *English Grammar in Use* (CUP.)
(A combination of reference grammar and exercises for intermediate
students.)

## 3  DICTIONARIES

*Collins Cobuild Essential English Dictionary* (Collins.)
*Oxford Advanced Learner's Dictionary of English* (OUP.)
*Longman Dictionary of Contemporary English* (Longman.)

## 4  SOURCES OF INFORMATION AND CONTACTS

### The British Council
The British Council represents Britain's cultural interests overseas.
There are about 80 British Council Offices throughout the world.
In many countries the British Council has a library.
Sometimes there are cultural events and concerts, as well as classes for students of English.
Your local British Council Office can tell you about the services available.
It can also supply you with a list of language schools in Britain.

### The BBC
The BBC World Service broadcasts to many countries.
BBC English by Radio broadcasts programmes for learners and teachers of English as a Foreign Language at all levels. For information about the BBC in your part of the world contact your local British Council Office; The Information Section of the British Embassy or write to:
BBC English by Radio & Television
PO Box 76
Bush House
Strand
London WC2B 4PH